MW01141924

Testimonials

"This is the perfect book for the community layperson as well as local government leaders and first responders. Bill Cooper uses his education and experience to provide critical subject matter in a post-9/11 citizens' guidebook of awareness, rivaling many training opportunities available only to law enforcement."   --Ryan Long, Police Officer

"Bill Cooper is one of the top terrorism experts in the US. His lectures are riveting. He clearly brings into perspective the threat of radical Islamic terrorism. Suicide Terror: Confronting the Threat is a must read for anyone serious about understanding this enemy."
                    --Captain Doug Roulstone, USN (ret)

"WOW! What an eye opener. Can't thank you enough for taking the time to be our guest speaker at the Evergreen Chapter, 1st Mar Div Association meeting. It has become apparent that most Americans fail to believe we are at WAR and there are fanatics who are out to KILL US ALL! I only hope your powerful message is reaching others in our communities and that you are not just preaching to the choir.
                    --Boyce Clark, USMC (ret)

"Personally, I think your presentation was outstanding and exactly on point ~ A Wake-Up Call To All! I too am a retired law enforcement professional with executive-level security and investigative business experience. I have significant parallel expertise in your field and I deeply appreciate and applaud your efforts with this troubling subject matter."
                    --Dave Munro, Citizen

Suicide Terror

Confronting the Threat

by William E. Cooper
Chief of Police (ret)

First Edition

3-Star Publishing
Mukilteo, WA   USA
425-275-7665
www.RealityOfTerrorism.com

3-Star Publishing
Mukilteo, WA USA
425-275-7665
www.realityofterrorism.com

ISBN 978-0-9767461-6-4
Printed in the United States of America

Cover Design by: MDM, Inc., Carmichael CA

Suicide Terror

Confronting the Threat

by William E. Cooper
Chief of Police (ret)

First Edition

3-Star Publishing
Mukilteo, WA   USA
425-275-7665
www.RealityOfTerrorism.com

Table of Contents

Dedication

This book is dedicated not only to the very fine first responders in America – the police, fire fighters, and emergency medical services – but to the millions of Americans who are concerned about the future of our country. Their concerns are real, yet through their vigilance and response, terrorist attacks have been prevented and untold numbers of lives saved.

It is because they are Americans, because they care about the country, their neighbors, friends and families that we have been successful. Yet the threat continues and is real. It will take the combined efforts of our great people to ultimately mitigate the problem. Americans believe they can make a difference, and do. They deserve the best officials, the best response capabilities, and the best results. They have earned it.

Bill Cooper trains groups of people about terrorists on a weekly basis.

About the Author

Bill Cooper retired as Chief of Police after nearly 30 years from a city near Seattle. Following the terrorist attacks of 9/11, Chief Cooper developed a series of terrorism response plans, and continues to train public and private sector organizations throughout the country.

Chief Cooper is the author of First Responders Guide to Terrorist Attacks, and co-author of the upcoming book Confronting Suicide Terror and is a certified Anti-Terrorism Specialist. In addition, he has investigated terrorism cases for a major transnational corporation, and has studied terrorism in the years following 9/11. He has attended numerous courses and seminars and is experienced in the intelligence field.

Chief Cooper holds an MBA and a second Masters Degree in Public Administration. He is a graduate of the FBI National Academy and the Washington State Law Enforcement Executive Command College. In addition, he is the author of the award-winning book, Leading Beyond Tradition. He teaches and consults in the areas of Building High Performance Organizations, Organizational Development, and Leadership. He is a Motorola trained Six Sigma Black Belt.

Acknowledgements

It is with profound gratitude that I acknowledge the following people for their contributions to this work. First, I'd like to thank Earl Johnson, my friend, and a survivor of the 9/11 attack on the World Trade Center, for his inspirational input to me in this endeavor, and for his teaming in a number of professional speaking engagements together. Second, and certainly of no little importance, has been my friendship with and the contributions of Captain Doug Roulstone, US Navy (ret). This man's insight and wisdom is truly significant.

I need to also acknowledge the contributions and mentorship of Jim Dyment, Seattle Police Department (ret). His work within the terrorism field and his guidance was exceptionally useful. And, a great friend and mentor, Bob Mahoney, retired FBI agent and Port Authority New York and New Jersey, who shared his experiences from the World Trade Center on 9/11 and the months of investigation that followed. I am deeply in his debt for all he's done for me.

I need to mention Adam Fosson, a dedicated and well informed man regarding international terrorism, with an emphasis on suicide terror. His thoughts proved exceptionally useful, and I appreciate his efforts and kindness. I also want to take a moment to acknowledge all the fine law enforcement officers, fire fighters, and emergency medical personnel in American, and elsewhere, who dedicate themselves to our safety. And to the American men and women serving in our military who are protecting us, a profound thank you. We are always in your debt. To

12
Steve McLaughlin, not only a friend and mentor, but recently retired as a Commander from the US Navy, I say thank you for your friendship and graciousness.

Finally, I want to thank my wife Patty. Without her help, patience, and guidance, this, and all the other works I've completed would not have come to fruition. She is the real idea person, and her tireless devotion and energy are the real catalysts for this book. Without her thoughtfulness, her encouragement, and her incisive thinking, this work would not have been produced. Thank you.

Foreword

When my friend Bill Cooper asked me write an introduction to his latest work, Suicide Terror: Confronting the Threat, I was both flattered and a bit concerned that I wouldn't know what to say. However, after some considerable reflection on my own direct experience as a recipient of a suicide terror attack I believe that I know exactly what to say.

Nothing strikes at the heart of civilized people more than the gruesome reality that among our fellow man exists a belief system that not only allows for, but actually encourages, supports and glorifies the act of the suicide terror attack. We find it naturally abhorrent that there are those among us, who feel it there duty to not merely take their own life in pursuit of their beliefs, but to do so in a manner that also kills as many others as possible that do not share their beliefs.

Americans in particular are poorly equipped to accept this reality as we have historically been merely observers from afar; witnessing for decades, these barbarous acts of religious based and politically motivated murder through the lens of the evening news. The fact that this distance driven detachment from reality hasn't been significantly changed by either the first attempt in 1993 to bring down the World Trade Center in New York, or the ultimately successful attack of 9/11 via commercial aircraft as human guided missiles, frankly scares me to death.

As a 51st Floor, North Tower survivor of the 9/11 massacre of innocent civilian life, I am profoundly troubled specifically at America's, and the West's in general, continued lack of understanding and at times even interest in the most rudimentary knowledge of the perpetrators beliefs and stated objectives.

I suppose much of it stems from the inability to even relate to the desire to die, let alone the motivations and world view of the Suicide Terrorist. We, as Americans, are after all born and raised within mankind's most tolerant and successful experiment to date, based upon the beliefs and practices that all men are created equal and that out of the many origins of our individual ancestries comes one people, united in beliefs surrounding freedom of religion, thought and expression. We have been conditioned to think passively and avoid conflict as we strive to live our lives peacefully, earn a living and raising our children.

This book is an indispensable resource in the effort to sound the alarm and awaken our collective slumber of indifference to the forces of evil that are planning today, the Suicide Terror of tomorrow. Unless and until we all can see the world as it is and not as we wish it, we will all be increasingly vulnerable to the death and destruction wrought by adherents to a philosophy of intolerance, hatred and death.

Earl C. Johnson

Disclaimer

This book contains information which may be thought to be offensive. The religion of Islam and the beliefs some of its followers will be discussed, this book is not intended to offend or criticize any particular group or faith unless specifically stated otherwise. Every effort has been made to insure the information presented is accurate. Extensive use has been made of documents and statements provided to media and other outlets. However, given the nature of the topic, and inability to verify all information, the author apologizes in advance for any errors and omissions.

Suicide Terror

Chapter 1
Introduction

Given the events of September 11, 2001, and the involvement of the United States domestically and internationally, international terrorism remains a high level threat to the United States. There is a widely held set of beliefs that terrorism is a relatively recent phenomenon, starting in recent decades. Precious little information is presented to Americans other than through the occasional book or paper, and often there are arguments to the contrary. No reasonable person believes that additional attacks will not occur in America.

Still Unanswered Questions

So, what is the reality of terrorism? How did it start? Is there a global effort by radical terrorists to spread their hatred? Can the terrorists be beaten? What will it take? A brief lesson for the people of the United States is necessary. Only by presenting an historical perspective can we truly get our arms around this problem and understand the nature and scope of what we are confronting.

Radical fundamentalist terrorism as we know it has been in existence for more than 1,400 years and we, as a society are largely unaware of what it is and why it exists, much less why the United States is being targeted. There is a belief by some that the presence of the US in other countries is precipitating the violence. Others believe that we inappropriately invaded another country (Iraq) causing new and more hatred of the United States and that we have done this before. More believe that the violence is about oil. There are widely disparate opinions available, but the truth of the matter has not largely been made available to the American public. All these opinions are beyond the scope of this work.

How Islamism Started

Some 1,400 years ago (610 AD) Mohammed, who lived in Mecca, Saudi Arabia, returned home one evening and told his wife he had been visited by the Angel Gabriel. He told her the angel said to him there was no God but Allah, and that Mohammed was his messenger. Mohammed then spent the next decade attempting to convert the citizens of Mecca to the new religion, Islam. At the time Mecca was largely a polytheistic society and Mohammed was not able to accomplish his goal, leaving Mecca not of his choice.

Killing and Destroying Was the Mission Then and Now

In 622 AD Mohammed migrated north to the city of Medina and spent the next several years converting that city to Islam, and assumed the leadership role. Because of the adversity he experienced in Mecca he began attacking caravans between the cities, followed by his decision to return to Mecca and capture it, which effort was successful. Many of the residents of Mecca were enslaved or killed if they refused to convert to Islam. During these years the Koran was being compiled as were the words of the prophet (Mohammed). Much of the content was dedicated to Islam becoming the one true religion on earth, using force if necessary.

Over the next 14 centuries a series of wars and conflicts occurred, resulting in the creation of Islamic empires, at one point stretching from Spain across southern Europe, Northern Africa, across the Middle East, India, and into Indonesia. This was defined as the righteous caliphate. These empires had not been established through peaceful processes, and attempts, successful or not were made to push them out of these regions.

One example involved the 200 years of the Crusades. Due to the extent of the empire, the Crusades were formed to push them back to the Middle East, which was accomplished over the 200-year period. Because of the violence of the wars, innocents were at times killed or injured and cities and villages looted. Today, when the Islamists speak of Crusaders they refer to that place in time.

Increasing the Violence

The most recent Islamic empire – the Ottoman Empire – ended after World War 1. During the war the empire allied itself with the Axis Powers, and with their defeat the League of Nations made the decision to remove the Islamic states and give them mostly to the British and French. It was after this that the Islamic scholars and jurists started to become more radical in their teachings, that the need for more aggressive approaches was necessary to re-establish Islam and the empire. One example is the Muslim Brotherhood, which was established in 1928, with more violent intentions.

Other than local incidents, little was actually accomplished towards those goals. Following the Second World War, the United Nations created the state of Israel (1948) within then Palestine, reducing Palestine's geography, which re-ignited Islamic fundamentalism. In order to create Israel, some 800,000 Palestinians migrated from the new Israel into the surrounding countries, including Syria, Lebanon, Jordan, and Egypt. These people argued they had lived in Palestine for 1,000 years, and the argument in return was that the Jews had Israel before they were forced out. The large numbers of refugees caused these nations to destabilize both economically and physically. They objected to the new Israel and attacked it, losing to Israel and losing additional geography (Gaza Strip, the West Bank, and Golan Heights). In the succeeding years a series of short wars occurred, with Israel usually winning.

Violence as Part of Islamic Fundamentalism

During the 1950's, 1960's, and 1970's, in addition to the wars, attacks, assassinations, bombings, and other violence occurred. This violence was typically confined to the Middle East, with the occasional incident in surrounding countries. The teachings by ever more radical jurists and imams (Islamic scholars and leaders – these are the leaders who interpret the Koran and create the path Muslims follow) continued. In 1979, two events occurred that re-awakened the Islamic fundamentalism to a new level, giving confidence to this growing segment of the Islamic religion.

The first was the invasion of Afghanistan by the Soviet Union. The 40th Army of the Soviet Union invaded, using their high tech MiG fighter planes, tanks, and other advanced weaponry. The Islamic residents of the country placed a global call for fighters to repel the Soviets, and many thousands responded. They were poorly equipped and organized for the fight, yet were able to succeed, in part because of training and equipment supplied by the United States. For ten years the war was engaged and ultimately the Soviets were pushed out of Afghanistan. The fighters learned lessons from the war – specifically that if you are committed and willing to die, you can beat a military superpower. They did not, however, believe that any power on earth could defeat the United States militarily.

The second event was the takeover of the US embassy in Tehran, Iran, and taking of American hostages, by the Ayatollah Khomeini after the Shah left the country. These hostages were held for 444 days without an American response, other than a failed rescue mission that left several members of the military dead after a crash. There was a belief among the radicals that Allah was strengthening their cause following these events. In 1980, when President Reagan was sworn in, the hostages were release.

However, the war in Afghanistan continued into the late 1980's, with the mujahedeen (warriors) ultimately victorious. One leader of the fighters, who helped fund and train fighters, was Osama bin Laden. As the war was coming to an end, bin Laden recognized there were a large number of trained and equipped fighters available, so he established al Qaeda (The Base), from which it was his intent to form a global Islamic army. He began to turn his sights to the US and Israel.

Chapter 2

Consequence of Suicide Terror

*"It is said that if you know your enemies
and know yourself, you will not be imperiled
in a hundred battles; if you do not know your
enemies but do know yourself, you will win
one and lose one; if you do not know your
enemies nor yourself, you will be imperiled
in every single battle."*

--Sun Tzu, 6th Century BC, The Art of War

New, Improved and Creative Bombings

The FBI and Department of Homeland Security agree that the probability of improvised explosive devices (IEDs) is an ongoing and ever increasing threat to the United States. Such devices, both human and vehicle borne, have continued to evolve and create significant damage and destruction in Iraq, and are likely to travel to America. These devices, with suicidal attackers, are a simplified version of a "smart bomb", that can be guided directly to its intended target, or change its path at any given moment to another target. These suicide bombers can select targets at will, and deliver themselves at a time of their choosing.

For law enforcement and citizens as well, both stopping them before they happen and responding to them after the detonation, present significant challenges. This chapter is designed to articulate the threat, and provide responders with basic tools to interdict the threat, or properly react after an attack happens.

Consequences if We Don't Act

Before the problem can be addressed there must be an understanding not only what the threat is, but what the consequences of failing to deal with it are. Americans, particularly law enforcement, are acutely aware of the attacks on the United States on 9/11, and the significant loss of life to families, friends, fellow Americans, and in the first responder community.

One of the most important questions Americans must ask is whether or not they are prepared for another, possibly more substantial attack? In many cases Americans are not prepared, the threat is in the past, they won't be the target, or they are just too busy with their lives, or may simply not recognize the true nature of those who wish us harm. An exploration of the initial step in identifying the true nature of the threat is in order.

10,000 Terrorist Attacks Since 9/11

There are few Americans who don't believe more attacks are coming, that it is a matter of when, not if. On the other hand, there are few who truly understand the extent to which those who wish the United States harm are prepared to go. Virtually everyone is familiar with Osama bin Laden and his ongoing series of threats, but many believe he is isolated or dead and unable to carry out future attacks.

There are other examples of terrorist threats, most of which draw little attention. The reality of these threats is that since 9/11 there have been more than 9,000 terrorist attacks, many in the Middle East and other parts of the globe not in close proximity to America. In addition, direct threats have been frequently made towards the United States, any of which are possible to carry out. The intent of terrorism, besides to casualties and economic loss, is to create psychological effects that go beyond the attack itself. The attacks on 9/11, years later, continue to have that impact.

National Intelligence Estimates

The unclassified version of the July 2007 National Intelligence Estimate states the following:

"We judge the US Homeland will face a persistent and evolving terrorist threat over the next three years. The main threat comes from Islamic terrorist groups and cells, especially al Qaeda, driven by their undiminished intent to attack the Homeland and a continued effort by these terrorist groups to adapt and improve their capabilities.

"al Qaeda can and will remain the most serious terrorist threat to the Homeland, as its central leadership continues to continues to plan high impact plots, which pushing others in extremist Sunni communities to mimic its efforts and to supplement its capabilities. al Qaeda will intensify its efforts to put operatives here.

"We assess that al Qaeda will continue to enhance its capabilities to attack the Homeland through greater cooperation with regional terrorist groups.

While We Have "Moved On" They Continue Plotting Against Us

"We assess that al Qaeda's Homeland plotting is likely to continue to focus on prominent political, economic, and infrastructure targets with the goal of producing mass casualties, visually dramatic destruction, significant economic aftershocks, and/or fear among the US population. The group is proficient with conventional small arms and improvised explosive devices, and is innovative in creating new capabilities and overcoming security obstacles.

"We assess that al Qaeda will continue to try to acquire and employ chemical, biological, radiological, or nuclear material in attacks and would not hesitate to use them if it develops what it deems is sufficient capability.

"We assess Lebanese Hizballah, which has conducted anti-US attacks outside the United States in the past, may be more likely to consider attacking the Homeland over the next three years if it perceives the United States as posing a direct threat to the group or Iran.

"We assess that the spread of radical – especially Salafi – Internet sites, increasingly aggressive anti-US rhetoric and actions, and the growing number of radical, self-generating cells in Western countries, indicate that the radical and violent segment of the West's Muslim population is expanding, including in the United States.

"We assess that other, non-Muslim terrorist groups, often referred to as 'single issue' groups by the FBI, probably will conduct attacks over the next three years given their violent histories.

"We assess that globalization trends and recent technological advances will continue to enable even small numbers of alienated people to find and connect with one another, justify and intensify their anger, and mobilize resources to attack – all without requiring a centralized terrorist organization, training camp, or leader."[1]

Examples of such threats include recent statements not only by terrorist group leaders, but state leaders:

Iranian President Mahmoud Ahmadinejad

"To those who doubt, to those who ask is it possible, or those who do not believe, I say accomplishment of a world without America and Israel is both possible and feasible."

Iranian Supreme Leader Ayatollah Ali Khamenei"

"The world of Islam has been mobilized against America for the past 25 years. The people call, "Death to America". Who used to say "Death to America?" who, besides the Islamic Republic and the Iranian people used to say this? Today everyone says this."

Hassan Abbassi, Revolutionary Guards Intelligence Advisor to the Iranian President

"We have a strategy drawn up for the destruction of Anglo-Saxon civilization ....we must make use of everything we have at hand to strike at this front by means of our suicide operations or by means of our missiles. There are 29 sensitive sites in the US and in the West. We have already spied on these sites, and we know how we are going to attack them."

Iraqi Ayatollah Ahmad Husseni

"If the objective circumstances materialize, and subjective there are soldiers, weapons, and money – even if this means using biological, chemical, and bacterial weapons – we will conquer the world, so that 'There is no God but Allah, and Muhammad is the Prophet of Allah' will be triumphant over the domes of Moscow, Washington, and Paris."

Venezuelan President Hugo Chavez

Chavez has called on Iran to "save the human race, let's finish off the US empire."

Osama bin Laden

"Kill the Americans and their allies, civilian and military. It is an individual duty for every Muslim who can do it in any country in which it is possible to do it."

Abu Ubeid al Qurashi

"al Qaeda takes pride in that, on 11 September it

destroyed elements of America's strategic defense, which the former USSR and every other hostile state could not harm. In addition to the destruction, al Qaeda has dealt America the most severe blow ever to their morale. The best means of bringing about a psychological defeat is to attack a place where the enemy feels safe and secure."

Ayman al Zawahiri

"The need to inflict the maximum casualties against the opponent, for this is the language understood by the West, no matter how much time and effort such operations take."

al Qaeda Manual

"Islamic governments have never and will never be established through peaceful solutions and cooperative councils. They are established as they (always) have been by pen and gun by word and bullet by tongue and teeth."

"We WILL Kill You..."

Having read these few of the many examples of the threats facing the United States, the simplest question for those who may doubt the intent is to ask, "What part of we're going to kill you doesn't the American population understand"? Literally tens of thousands of people have been killed in these types of attacks and many thousands more injured. Of note is that the largest single terrorist event in history occurred in the United States, and comes with promises of more to follow.

Stratfor (Strategic Forecasting) stated in its July 25, 2007 report that, "As long as the ideology of jihadism exists and jihadists embrace the philosophy of attacking 'the far enemy', they will pose a threat on US soil. There are likely homegrown and transnational jihadists in the United States right now plotting attacks. We believe the United States is long overdue for an attack".[2]

It is therefore imperative that the American people not only know and understand the threat, but understand the philosophies, strategies, and tactics employed that will be used to carry them out. It is also essential that people know they have been targeted and can react to a terrorist attack. Citizens must know and understand these enemies before they can be defeated.

Chapter 3

Interdicted Attacks in the US

They Have Tried Since 9/11

Americans should take particular note that a number of terrorist attacks have been prevented in the United States prior to and since 9/11, further ratifying the true threat to our country. While there has been some information released, the useful details of these potentially damaging attacks have not largely been shared. Because of alert citizens and law enforcement working together several of these attacks were prevented. Some examples of interdicted attacks include:

- **1999 – Ahmed Ressam – the "Millennium Bomber"**

Ressam was attempting to transport explosives into the United States to explode at Los Angeles International Airport to mark the millennium. He was arrested due to the observance of US Customs officers.

- **2001 – Richard Reid– the "Shoe Bomber"**

Reid attempted to blow up a trans-Atlantic commercial jet by detonating explosives in his shoe. He was stopped due to an alert flight attendant.

- **2002 – Jose Padilla**

Padilla was arrested returning to the US after training with alleged intent of blowing up apartment buildings using natural gas, and allegedly to detonate "dirty bombs" in the US.

• 2003 – Majid Khan

Khan allegedly intended to target US bridges, gas stations, including underground tanks, and poison water reservoirs.

• 2003 – Iyman Faris

Faris was involved in determining the probability of downing the Brooklyn Bridge and derailing passenger trains.

• 2004 – Herald Square, NY

Plotted to use suicide bombers to collapse Manhattan Mall. Attackers had previously discussed NYPD precincts on Staten Island and the Verazzano Bridge.

• 2004 – Dhiren Barot

Barot and his team plotted attacks both in the United States and the United Kingdom. Targets in the US included the International Monetary Fund, World Bank, New York Stock Exchange, Citigroup Headquarters, and the Prudential Building. Attacks involved the use of vehicles containing explosives.

• 2005 – Shayk Shahaab Murshid

He targeted US military facilities, the Israeli Consulate, and Jewish synagogues in Los Angeles. Interdicted due to local law enforcement action.

• 2006 – "Miami Seven"

Targeted Sears Tower in Chicago and conducted

surveillance of Miami Police Department, Federal Justice Building, FBI Building, courthouses, and the federal Detention center.

• 2006 – Derrick Shareef

Targeted a mall in Rockford, Illinois at Christmas time.

• 2006 – Khaled Sheik Mohammad

At Guantanamo Bay, he stated he had planned more than 30 attacks, including several in the United States.

• 2007 – Fort Dix plot

Six members of local group targeted Fort Dix military base for an attack. Intended to enter the base and kill as many soldiers as possible before escaping. Interdicted due to observant citizen.

• 2007 – JFK Airport plot

Four members of local group intended to blow up fuel deport and fuel lines for JFK airport, causing massive damage and many casualties.

As may be seen there actually have been attempts to attack the Homeland on multiple occasions, and Americans should be aware of the methodologies used in planning and preparing to execute the attacks. It also provides significant evidence that the Homeland will be attacked again, perhaps on multiple occasions, using multiple strategies. Understanding the attackers provides our people with the ability to examine possibilities and probabilities to know strategies regarding stopping an attack occur.

Who Are They – Really?

It is simply a matter of understanding who the attackers are and what and how they think and believe. Time Magazine printed an article on July 4th, 2005 entitled "Inside the Mind of a Suicide Bomber". The article involved the interview of a suicide bomber waiting for the call to conduct his attack. He is quoted here to demonstrably show the seriousness of the threat of such incidents coming to the United States.

> *"First I will ask Allah to bless my mission*
> *with a high rate of casualties among the*
> *Americans. The most important thing is*
> *that he should let me kill many Americans."*[3]

Further evidence of terrorist activities in the United States may be found in the identification of terror cells in Virginia, New Jersey, Oregon, New York and two cities in California. These do not include the cells or groups discussed elsewhere in this chapter. It is clear that the threat is here and as time passes potentially becomes more imminent. Citizens must take note and prepare accordingly.

Detection of Key Terrorist Activities

Having this information in mind, the next step is to examine how to detect key terrorist activities. What are those things a terrorist or group is doing that may assist law enforcement in detecting their actions? How does a terrorist attack occur, and can it be stopped? One of the best systems to utilize, and one being used across the country is entitled The Seven Steps of Terrorism. History has shown that the planning, preparation, and execution of an attack typically follow these seven steps. Through an understanding of these steps, interdiction of an attack is possible during any one of them.

No State Left Out

As previously stated, it is well known and documented that there are terrorist sleeper cells in the United States, from Florida to Washington State, New York to California, Illinois to Texas. It is unreasonable to expect or believe there are not others being planned or developed.

While Law Enforcement Plans, Terrorists Carefully Prepare

Law enforcement continues to develop information and intelligence sharing capabilities that has significantly enhanced their ability to identify and track terrorist members of these cells. With these abilities, and the growing cooperation of the public, opportunities to recognize potential targets, potential terrorists, and likely methods of attack is increasing. Through education of the people, they are learning to combat fear and apprehension through action, by emphasizing safety, understanding, and preparation.

One major element is for us to understand what the terrorists have done and how they carry out their plans. Historically, they are meticulous planners, and seem to be in no hurry to launch an attack unless and until they are ready. They spend considerable time and effort gathering information in order to maximize the effect of an attack.

Expect Bombs

The weapon of choice tends to be explosives, frequently by means of suicide bombers. They use IED's (Improvised Explosive Devices) and VBIED's (Vehicle Borne Improvised Explosive Devices) as the most common explosive approaches. Their knowledge and use of these devices is growing through experiences in Iraq and other countries. Terrorists use a methodological approach for planning and executing attacks.

The Department of Homeland Security prepared and distributed an information guide titled The Seven Signs of Terrorism; the guide is an accurate representation of the strategies employed by terrorists. These Seven Signs offer an opportunity to look for unusual circumstances and report them to law enforcement. The benefit to all Americans is that at any one of these steps, a potential attack can be prevented.

Sign 1 – Surveillance

Prior to an attack, often weeks or months before, terrorists will conduct surveillance and scouting operations. Such methods include photography, videotapes, diagramming, mapping, measuring, and observing security, or other out of the ordinary practices. These acts have occurred on our ferry systems in New York and Washington State, the JFK airport, power grids, dams, buildings (Sears Tower in Chicago), bridges (Brooklyn and George Washington in New York), tunnels (Lincoln and Holland in New York), subway systems, rail, and many others.

What to look for:

- Suspicious people taking video or photos, diagramming or measuring in areas not normal; they may be there on multiple occurrences, or may be different people collecting the same information; staying in position for longer than normal times.

- The use of technology such as cell phone cameras, mini-cameras.

- Taking photos or video of security; timing security, measuring distances from police or fire stations to the target.

- The use of GPS units where it seems unusual.

- People in possession of maps of critical infrastructure, highlighted in key areas.

• The use of communications equipment where not normally used – cell phones, walkie-talkies.

For example, in Washington State, there has been considerable surveillance done on the ferry system. Hundreds of reports have been made of suspicious activities, including photography, videotaping, measuring, diagramming, cell phone conversations with nearby boats, attempts to enter secure areas, including the pilot house and engine rooms. The photography has not been of the truly outstanding scenery of Seattle, but has been of structural supports of the ferries, security operations, traffic and passenger movement, and ferry operations. Many of these cases have been reported to law enforcement and investigations determined that more than two dozen were classified as pre-operational surveillance.

Other examples have included surveillance of similar activities in shopping malls, mass transportation, power stations, cell towers, dams, and other critical facilities. There are many well documented cases of such behavior in the United States. As will be discussed in a later chapter, there have been a number of attacks disrupted in America due to citizens and law enforcement personnel who are alert and aware.

Sign 2 – Elicitation

Terrorists will attempt to gather and obtain information about a place, person, or operation that is more likely than not a critical infrastructure, either public or private. They may ask questions, make inquiries, they may obtain plans or blueprints, or other information, much of it from the Internet.

What to look for:

- People asking questions, unusual or normal, looking to get information. Pay particular attention to questions about security, access to facilities or information systems, delivery schedules.

- Attempts to access information via computer – blueprints, plans, schedules, anything to do with strengths or weaknesses. Information in the media has been of interest.

An example of elicitation may involve a person unknown to you, asking what may appear to be normal questions, always looking for information. Such a case may involve a critical facility, such as a power station, or computer data center. The person may appear as if a tourist or just a person interested in electronics or computers. Questions may include hours of operation, how many people work in the building, whether it has security, or alarm systems to protect the facility or business information. These questions may be fitted in among other ordinary conversation. Always be aware that if it doesn't seem normal, it probably isn't.

Sign 3 – Tests of Security

Terrorists will test security/law enforcement by entering or attempting to enter secured or essential facilities or locations, and/or will time responses and routes of response. The locations of police, fire, emergency medical services will be identified and routes of response located; timing of response likely will happen as well, usually through a false alarm.

What to look for:

- People attempting to enter secured or forbidden areas. If contacted by security while doing so, they will usually have a plausible story.

- Attempts to move prohibited materials through security to determine if they will be detected and what the response will be.

- False alarm or false report of an incident to test response times, deployment, and numbers of responders.

- Testing of alarm systems to determine reaction and timing.

- Unattended packages or briefcases to see what the reaction will be.

There are any number of examples supporting this as a planning step. On the Washington State ferries, for example, there were many attempts to enter the locked engineering facilities or locked pilot house. These attempts have been both overt and covert. Each time, when caught doing so, there is always a prepared story for the particular circumstances.

Another case occurred at a major shopping mall where the suspicious behavior involved the attempt to enter secure areas. The intent is to try to determine what the response by security, law enforcement, or store personnel would be, always looking for the amount of time it takes to react, as well as what the actual reaction will be. Again, when contacted, there is always a prepared story to be told.

Sign 4 – Acquiring Supplies

Terrorists will purchase weapons and ammunition, explosives or the components of explosives, chemicals, equipment, or military or law enforcement identification and uniforms to allow easier access into areas.

What to look for:

- People who buy excessive amounts of dangerous chemicals or components that can be used in constructing explosive devices – an example would be fertilizer (ammonium nitrate).

- People buying weapons and ammunition at unusual levels.

- People who are not law enforcement or security buying (or stealing) uniforms, badges, identification cards.

- People buying used emergency vehicles that may be used in an effort to access the target without raising suspicion.

- People attempting to obtain access cards to facilities.

- Thefts of weapons, with an emphasis on military grade weapons.

In recent years, there have been a number of thefts of law enforcement vehicles, ambulances, and government vehicles. There are also a number of cases of stolen or missing law enforcement, fire, and emergency medical personnel uniforms, badges, and identification cards. Many have not been recovered, and it is not known if terrorists stole them. Presuming they did in some cases, an emergency vehicle or uniform, including identification can offer any number of opportunities to enter into areas not normally accessible.

Weapons are easy to obtain, as is ammunition. Explosives and explosive components are no longer that easy to purchase in quantity due to the highly successful efforts of law enforcement. Due to the awareness of the American people it has become much more difficult to amass large quantities of potentially dangerous materials for use in an attack. Of note is that we must remain diligent in being aware, prepared, and need to report.

Sign 5 – Suspicious People

Look for people who are out of the ordinary, who do not belong, or whose actions are out of the ordinary. Appearance, position, and actions may each be indicators. This may be as simple as knowing it when you see it – to follow your instincts. Profile behaviors, not people. Terrorists take advantage of political correctness and the fear of potentially offending someone.

Terrorists are not all of one race, color, or gender. They use men, women, and children of many races and ages. There are numerous cases of these actions, including parents placing explosives on their children and exploding them in crowds. There are cases of terrorists placing explosives on the elderly and mentally handicapped people, then directing them to the target and exploding them. Watch for suspicious behaviors, not suspicious people. If it looks wrong, it may very well be wrong – report it.

What to look for:

- People whose actions are not ordinary or normal.
- People who seem out of place.
- People not dressed for the weather or location.
- People trying to avoid detection or letting others see who they are.
- People who are evasive when spoken to or confronted.
- Carrying materials not suitable to the location.
- People attempting to hide.
- Reports of weapons practice in out of the way areas.

Because the American people are substantially more aware of events, circumstances, and their surroundings, detecting these activities is much more frequent. Passengers on Washington State ferries report many suspicious behaviors. The recent case in New Jersey involving the terrorists plotting to attack Fort Dix was stopped due to an alert store clerk reporting behaviors on a video.

A case in Washington State involved neighbors observing long-time neighbors with their garage full of cases of cigarettes. Although they did not know of the significance, this inquiry led the FBI to money laundering for terrorists through cigarette purchases, which is not an uncommon tactic to raise money. Other than the cigarettes these next door neighbors were friendly and sociable people.

Sign 6 – Dry Runs

Prior to the actual attack the terrorists will conduct one or more dry runs to look for flaws or unanticipated problems. This is a critical time when they may be identified or caught. There are many examples of this occurring. Prior to 9/11 the hijackers flew on the same planes they ultimately hijacked on multiple occasions scouting the best seats, timing opening and closing cockpit doors, timing specific actions of flight attendants, which planes had the most fuel and fewest passengers, always looking to maximize casualties and damage.

The terrorists plotting to hijack 10 airliners out of the UK were identified and apprehended during a dry run.

Virtually all major attacks, before they occur, will have had at least one or more dry runs. Terrorists will conduct a test of their plan to look for problems they may overcome before the actual operation.

What to look for:

- Tests of the system: security, response times, reactions to the test.
- Suspicious people or suspicious actions – if they seem out of the ordinary they probably are.

Terrorist interest in airlines has not diminished, and they are continually seeking new ways to use aircraft as controlled missiles to specific targets. More recent dry runs have included using larger numbers of hijackers, different types of explosives, and theft of airline uniforms and identification. Actual attempts have been stopped in other countries, including a recent attempt in China.

The Fort Dix plotters made a number of runs into the fort delivering pizza in order to determine the best time, best route, and best escape route from the fort. From an elicitation perspective, as a result of prior business in the fort, they were able to obtain a map, ostensibly to know where to deliver the pizza – an excellent example of elicitation.

Sign 7 – Deployment of Assets

This is immediately prior to the attack and is the last opportunity to stop the attack. The terrorists will move into their pre-determined positions just prior to the attack. Once in place and the timing is appropriate, they will attack the target. The history of attacks demonstrates that the terrorists may not always assemble in one location. These are the activities where the terrorists stage for the attack.

What to look for:

- People or vehicles in unusual positions or places
- People dressed in clothing not aligned with weather or location.
- Unusual number of people or vehicles (or vehicle types) in vicinity of possible attack site.

While these indicators and signs are not a complete list, they give the reader an idea of what to look for and report, or respond to.

Chapter 4

The Suicide Bomber

Suicide terror, also known as martyrdom operations, involves an "individual who makes great sacrifices or suffers much in order to further a belief, cause, or principle" (www.answers.com). Adam Fosson, terrorism analyst, writes in his paper "The Globalization of Martyrdom: Cause and Effect" (July 2007) that in recruitment of suicide bombers, considerable planning is involved.

He writes that "One extremely crucial way these individuals are indoctrinated, trained, and recruited for martyrdom operations worldwide is through the Internet. It exploits the humiliation and anger sensed by many Muslims, while offering them an opportunity to make a difference."[4]

Fosson further writes that "Both religion and the humiliation of life under occupation are often key motives for suicide bombers seeking a better life in paradise."[5] Fosson's extensive research concluded, for example, that in Palestine, "the idea of a child wanting to become a martyr is nearly the same as an American child wanting to visit Disneyland".[6]

Fosson concludes his paper with an extremely insightful couple of statements, one which first responders and citizens should pay particular attention to as they plan and prepare. He states, "As time goes by, the only way to anticipate a possible martyrdom operation is to essentially use your imagination. The statement that the United States had a "failure of imagination" prior to September 11, 2001, is pertinent here. The US did not believe that an enemy such as al-Qaida, based thousands of miles away, could do harm to our homeland."[7]

Detection of Terrorist Recruitment in the Community

Recruitment of potential terrorist operatives, including suicide bombers, is an ongoing and global set of actions terrorist organizations are engaged in. One of the more frequently discussed reasons for recruits to join is the anger with the US for the war in Iraq.

The key for citizens, and law enforcement to dealing with terrorist recruitment in the community is two-fold:

1. Understand where and how recruitment is occurring;

2. Disrupt recruitment methods.

Terrorist operations require personnel, money, and materials, as well as places from which to work and to live. If Americans, as well as responders know how recruitment works for terrorists, they find themselves in a better position to interdict it. The basis for recruitment involves several elements, each of which presents an opportunity to identify and react. These elements include where terrorist groups recruit, how they recruit, who they target, and why those people are targeted.

Where they recruit:

1. The Internet – there are currently more than 5000 sites on the Internet of a jihadist nature. Particular segments of the population are identified and targeted – some accept and some do not. For those invited or who may seek out the site there may be an expectation of what the content is.

2. The use of videos and CDs. There has been an ongoing use of fairly high quality videos produced by al Qaeda and others that contain considerable anti-American rhetoric, designed, in part, to add to the number of people being recruited globally, including the United States.

3. Mosques may have the reputation for being "radical". For those attending, there may be an understanding of what would be expected. For some of those attending these mosques they may be seeking certain behaviors or philosophies they can align with. In a significant percentage of the more than 2,900 mosques in the United States there is no shortage of ever escalating anti-American rhetoric.

4. Law enforcement should look for ritualistic behaviors as recruiting gets underway. Such behaviors include "hazing rituals and group identity building exercises, or in the case of al Qaeda, validation of commitment to its principles through the recruit's demonstrated

knowledge of radical Islam and the use of violence to achieve its goals. These techniques can result in radically polarized and altered attitudes among those who successfully navigate them, usually along the lines desired by the recruiting group." [8]

5. Another way to target select members of a population is to infiltrate them. The infiltrator will recruit from within the group. Law enforcement should be aware of such groups in their communities which may be specifically targeted.

6. Colleges and universities – there are a number of professors and students at major US universities who subscribe to jihadist philosophies.

Terror candidates or operatives have entered the country using student visas. In some cases, these philosophies are openly taught.

Of note is that terrorists have scouted schools at all levels, from colleges and universities to pre-schools. The lessons of the Beslan siege certainly apply in the United States if the target of attack is a school. Americans may safely assume that all the school shootings have been studied and have been assessed by terrorists to determine the likelihood of a successful attack. The response of law enforcement and emergency medical services has likely been timed and deployments observed.

What they look for to recruit (Rand Report):

1. A high level of current distress or dissatisfaction (emotional, physical, or both);

2. Cultural disillusionment in a frustrated seeker (i.e., unfulfilled idealism)

3. Lack of an intrinsic religious belief system or value system

4. Some dysfunctionality in family system (i.e., family and kin exert "weak gravity")

5. Some dependent personality tendencies (e.g., suggestibility, low tolerance, or ambiguity)

For example, potential shoe bomber Richard Reid had four of the five traits listed above. When discussing anti-American sentiments, the "recruitment pitch is simple: American policies are directly responsible for Muslim misery, all over the world."[9]

Who is being recruited has changed considerably. Previously, suicide terrorists were younger Middle Eastern men. Now, terrorist organizations are recruiting men and women, various races and cultures, older and younger, and in some extreme cases have or will use small children to attack a target. Given the diverse society of America, intervention goals include identifying the recruiters and potential people targeted for recruiting. It is important that law enforcement have a good working relationship with its community, certainly sufficient to trust that potential recruiting centers, efforts, and recruit possibilities are reported.

Jails and prisons are one of the more common sources terrorist recruits are sought and make commitments to terrorist philosophies and acts. The majority of those incarcerated possess some, if not all, the characteristics previously discussed. John S. Pistole, Assistant Director of the FBI's Counterterrorism Division, testified before Congress in October, 2003 that US correctional facilities are a viable venue for radicalization and recruitment.

"Recruitment of inmates within the prison system will continue to be a problem for correctional institutions throughout the country. Inmates are often ostracized, abandoned by, or isolated from their family and friends, leaving them susceptible to recruitment. Membership in the various radical groups offer inmates protection, positions of influence and a network they can correspond with both inside and outside of prison."[10]

The *al Qaeda Manual* itself describes the characteristics of recruits they seek. While the list of traits is fairly extensive, parts of it are included here to provide law enforcement (and ultimately members of the community to be sought for assistance) the tools necessary to assist in identifying potential terrorist suicide operatives. This chapter makes extensive use of the *al Qaeda Manual* to provide the first responder the philosophies and strategies employed by the terrorists. The manual's second chapter is quoted here.

"Necessary Qualifications for the Organization's Members:

1. The member of the organization must be Moslem.

2. The member must be committed to the organization's ideals.

3. Maturity – the requirements of military work are numerous, and a minor cannot perform them. The nature of hard and continuous work in dangerous conditions requires a great deal of psychological, mental, and intellectual fitness.

4. Sacrifice – the member must be willing to do the work and undergo martyrdom for the purpose of achieving the goal and establishing the religion of majestic Allah on earth.

5. Listening and obedience – this is known today as discipline. It is expressed by how the member obeys the orders given to him.

6. Keeping secrets and concealing information – this secrecy should be used even with the closest people, for deceiving the enemies is not easy.

7. Free of illness – the military organization's member must fulfill this important requirement.

8. Patience – the member should have plenty of patience for enduring afflictions if he is overcome by the enemies. He should be patient in performing the work, even if it takes a long time.

9. Tranquility and unflappability – the member should have a calm personality that allows him to endure psychological traumas such as those involving bloodshed, murder, arrest, imprisonment, and reverse psychological traumas such as killing one or all of his organization's comrades. He should be able to carry out the work.

10. Intelligence and insight

11. Caution and prudence

12. Truthfulness and counsel

13. Ability to observe and analyze

14. Ability to act, change positions, and conceal oneself."[11]

Chapter 5

Identifying Safe Houses and Planning Centers

The al Qaeda manual provides first responders and American citizens with its blueprint for the selection and use of safe houses. This information is useful for law enforcement investigations and patrol operations. It is also use for fire and EMS in the event they respond to a fire or other incident at one of these locations. Each will have some awareness of the dangers and threats involved. The manual's fourth lesson is extensively quoted here.

"Security Precautions Related to Apartments:

1. Choosing the apartment carefully as far as the location, the size for the work necessary (meetings storage, arms, fugitives, work preparation).

2. It is preferable to rent apartments on the ground floor to facilitate escape.

3. Preparing secret locations in the apartment for securing documents, records, arms, and other important items.

4. Preparing ways of vacating the apartment in case of a surprise attack (stands, wooden ladders).

5. Under no circumstances should anyone know about the apartment other than those using them.

6. Providing the necessary cover for the people who frequent the apartment (students, workers, employees, etc.).

7. Avoiding seclusion and isolation from the population and refraining from going to the apartment at suspicious times.

8. It is preferable to rent these apartments using false names, appropriate cover, and non-Moslem appearance.

9. A single brother should not rent more than one apartment in the same area, from the same agent, or using the same rental office.

10. Care should be exercised not to rent apartments that are known to the security apparatus such as those used for immoral or prior Jihad activities.

11. Avoiding police stations and government buildings. Apartments should not be rented near these places.

12. When renting these apartments, one should avoid isolated or deserted locations so the enemy would not be able to catch those living there easily.

13. It is preferable to rent apartments in newly developed areas where people do not know one another. Usually, in older quarters people know one another and strangers are easily identified,

especially since these quarters have many informers.

14. Ensuring that there has been no surveillance prior to the members entering the apartment.

15. Agreement among those living in the apartment on special ways of knocking on the door and special signs prior to entry into the building's main gate to indicate to those who wish to enter that the place is safe and not being monitored. Such signs include hanging out a towel, opening a curtain, placing a cushion is a special way, etc.

16. If there is a telephone in the apartment, calls should be answered in an agreed upon manner among those who use the apartment. That would prevent mistakes that would otherwise lead to revealing the names and nature of the occupants.

17. For apartments, replacing the locks and keys with new ones. As for the other entities (camps, shops, mosques), appropriate security precautions should be taken depending on the entity's importance and role in the work.

18. Apartments used for undercover work should not be visible from higher apartments in order not to expose the nature of the work.

19. In a newer apartment, avoid talking loud because prefabricated ceilings and walls used in the apartments do not have the same thickness as those in old ones.

20. It is necessary to have at hand documents supporting the undercover member. In the case of a physician, there should be an actual medical diploma, membership in the medical union, the government permit, and the rest of the routine procedures used in that country.

21. The cover should blend well with the environment. For example, selecting a doctor's clinic in an area where there are clinics, or in a location suitable for it.

22. The cover of those who frequent the location should match the cover of that location. For example, a common laborer should not enter a fancy hotel because that would be suspicious and draw attention."[12]

First responders, in looking for or entering a bomb-making lab, should be aware of chemicals, explosives, and other bomb-making materials (pipes, electronic components, and computers – particularly laptops. These computers usually prove invaluable in terms of intelligence. Responders also should be aware of various chemical odors.

A case example involves the 1995 Operation Bojinka plots in the Philippines. Terrorists began a detailed and meticulous plot to assassinate the Pope while in the Philippines, and the destruction of as many as a dozen commercial airliners over the Pacific Ocean. The plot was discovered when a fire started in the terrorists' apartment in Manila while they constructed the small, but powerful explosive devices for the planes. As the fire spread the terrorists vacated the apartment. When the responders arrived and put out the fire they found a large number of items of evidentiary and intelligence value, as well as a laptop computer.

The computer contained detailed plans for the attacks, as well as identifying the planners. They recovered items associated with the plot to kill the Pope, including maps of the papal motorcade, pictures of the Pope, rosaries, and robes similar to the cassocks the priests would normally wear.

In addition, evidence of the plot to blow up as many as a dozen airliners was on the laptop. Chemicals in the apartment included various acids, ammonium nitrate, nitroglycerin, cylinders, fuses, and chemistry equipment. Completed pipe bombs were found, Casio watches to be used as explosive devices were present, a manual on building liquid-based bombs, and a number of falsified passports were also collected.

Also present on the laptop were the schedules of the flights to be destroyed, times of explosions aboard each aircraft, the names of numerous people associated with the group, as well as photographs, and a number of documents regarding anti-US and anti-Israel sentiments. To cap off the investigation, details and identities of the perpetrators of the first World Trade Center bombing were on the laptop – the same people preparing the bombs in the Bojinka case.

Americans should be aware of such evidence if they see such activities or events, and need to work closely with law enforcement by reporting the information as quickly as possible. People should also be aware the terrorists will go to extensive lengths to protect these locations.

Chapter 6

Terrorist Communications

Terrorist organizations use meticulous planning in all aspects of their operations. One of the key elements is their ability to communicate with one another. With the number of terror attacks worldwide the United States employed a number of technologies to intercept communications among the groups and cells. As a consequence, the terrorist organizations adapted and used other technologies, including the Internet.

Jihadist forums on the Internet are extensive and contain many hundreds of files on jihadist philosophies, strategies, and methods. Examining these files provides law enforcement and private sector security a wealth of information and data on which to base prevention, response, and mitigation strategies.

In addition, considerable training materials are shared across hundreds of Internet sites, said sites being disbanded when training is completed. Given that following 9/11 the United States destroyed the training camps in Afghanistan the Internet has become the vehicle for providing extensive levels and types of training. The terrorist can learn from the comfort of his home.

US efforts were successful in obtaining additional information, so again the terrorists adjusted their operations. Their communications strategy is clearly articulated in the al Qaeda Manual and much of that strategy is included here so law enforcement and community members understand the basics behind how information is passed among the groups. The key here is to understand that the terrorists are continually adapting and adjusting their methodologies to evade interdiction efforts. The communications portion of the manual is included here. The Fifth Lesson in the *al Qaeda Manual* is provided in part.

"Communication Means:

The Military Organization in any Islamic group can, with its modest capabilities, use the following means:

1. The telephone,
2. Meeting in-person,
3. Messenger,
4. Letters,
5. Some modern devices, such as the facsimile and wireless [communication].

Communication may be within the county, state, or even the country, in which case it is called local communication. When it extends expanded between countries, it is then called international communication.

Secret Communication is Limited to the Following Types:

Common, standby, alarm

1. Common Communication:
   It is a communication between two members of
   the Organization without being monitored by
   the security apparatus opposing the Organization. The common communication should be
   done under a certain cover and after inspecting
   the surveillance situation [by the enemy].

2. Standby Communication:
   This replaces common communication when
   one of the two parties is unable to communicate
   with the other for some reason.

3. Alarm Communication:
   This is used when the opposing security apparatus discovers an undercover activity or some
   undercover members. Based on this communication, the activity is stopped' for a while, all matters related to the activity are abandoned, and the
   Organization's members are hidden from the
   security personnel.

Method of Communication Among Members of the Organization:

1. Communication about undercover activity should be done using a good cover; it should also be quick, explicit, and pertinent. That is just for talking only.

2. Prior to contacting his members, the commander of the cell [B] should agree with each of them separately (the cell members should never meet all in one place and should not know one another) on a manner and means of communication with each other. Likewise, the chief of the organization should [use a similar technique] with the branch commanders.

   [B.] Cell or cluster methods should be adopted by the Organization. It should be composed of many cells whose members do not know one another, so that if a cell member is caught the other cells would not be affected, and work would proceed normally.

3. A higher-ranking commander determines the type and method of communication with lower-ranking leaders.

First Means: The Telephone

Because of significant technological advances, security measures for monitoring the telephone and broadcasting equipment have increased. Monitoring may be done by installing a secondary line or wireless broadcasting device on a telephone that relays the calls to a remote location...That is why the Organization takes security measures among its members who use this means of communication (the telephone).

1. Communication should be carried out from public places. One should select telephones that are less suspicious to the security apparatus and are more difficult to monitor. It is preferable to use telephones in booths and on main streets.

2. Conversation should be coded or in general terms so as not to alert the person monitoring [the telephone].

3. Periodically examining the telephone wire and the receiver.

4. Telephone numbers should be memorized and not recorded. If the brother has to write them, he should do so using a code so they do not appear as telephone numbers (figures from a shopping list, etc.)

5. The telephone caller and person called should mention some words or sentences prior to bringing up the intended subject. The brother who is calling may misdial one of the digits and actually call someone else. The person

'called may claim that the call is for him, and the calling brother may start telling him work-related issues and reveal many things because of a minor error.

6. In telephone conversations about undercover work, the voice should be changed and distorted.

7. When feasible, it is preferable to change telephone lines to allow direct access to local and international calls. That and proper cover facilitate communications and provide security protection not available when the central telephone station in the presence of many employees is used.

8. When a telephone [line] is identified [by the security apparatus], the command and all parties who were using it should be notified as soon as possible in order to take appropriate measures.

9. When the command is certain that a particular telephone [line] is being monitored, it can exploit it by providing information that misleads the enemy and benefits the work plan.

10. If the Organization manages to obtain jamming devices, it should use them immediately.

Second Means: Meeting in-person

This is direct communication between the commander and a member of the Organization. During the meeting the following are accomplished:

1. Information exchange,
2. Giving orders and instructions,
3. Financing,
4. Member follow-up

Stages of the In-Person Meeting

A. Before the meeting,
B. The meeting [itself],
C. After the meeting.

A. Before the Meeting:

1. The following measures should be taken:
1. **Designating the meeting location,**
2. **Finding a proper cover for the meeting,**
3. **Specifying the meeting date and time,**
4. **Defining special signals between those who meet.**

1. Identifying the meeting location:

If the meeting location is stationary, the following matters should be observed:

a. The location should be far from police stations and security centers.
b. Ease of transportation to the location.

c. Selecting the location prior to the meeting and learning all its details.

d. If the meeting location is an apartment, it should not be the first one, but one somewhere in the middle.

e. The availability of many roads leading to the meeting location. That would provide easy escape in case the location ware raided by security personnel.

f. The location should not be under suspicion (by the security [apparatus])

g. The apartment where the meeting takes place should be on the ground floor, to facilitate escape.

h. The ability to detect any surveillance from that location.

i. When public transportation is used, one should alight at some distance from the meeting location and continue on foot. In the case of a private vehicle, one should park it far away or in a secure place so as to be able to maneuver it quickly at any time.

If the meeting location is not stationary, the following matters should be observed:

i. The meeting location should be at the intersection of a large number of main and side streets to facilitate entry, exit, and escape.

ii. The meeting location (such as a coffee shop) should not have members that might be dealing with the security apparatus.

iii. The meeting should not be held in a crowded place because that would allow the security

personnel to hide and monitor those who meet.
iv. It is imperative to agree on an alternative location for the meeting in case meeting in the first is unfeasible. That holds whether the meeting place is stationary or not.

Those who meet in-person should do the following:

i. Verifying the security situation of the location before the meeting.
ii. Ensuring that there are no security personnel behind them or at the meeting place.
iii. Not heading to the location directly.
iv. Clothing and appearance should be appropriate for the meeting location.
v. Verifying that private documents carried by the brother have appropriate cover.
vi. Prior to the meeting, designing a security plan that specifies what the security personnel would be told in case the location were raided by them, and what [the brothers] would resort to in dealing with the security personnel (fleeing, driving back,...)

2. Finding a proper cover for the meeting: [The cover]

i. should blend well with the nature of the location.
ii. in case they raid the place, the security personnel should believe the cover.
iii. should not arouse the curiosity of those present.
iv. should match the person's appearance and

his financial and educational background.

v. should have documents that support it.

vi. provide reasons for the two parties' meeting (for example, one of the two parties should have proof that he is an architect. The other should have documents as proof that he is a land owner. The architect has produced a construction plan for the land).

3. Specifying the Meeting Date and Time

i. Specifying the hour of the meeting as well as the date.

ii. Specifying the time of both parties' arrival and the time of the first party's departure.

iii. Specifying how long the meeting will last.

iv. Specifying an alternative date and time.

v. Not allowing a long period of time between making the meeting arrangements and the meeting itself.

4. Designating special signals between those who meet.

If the two individuals meeting know one another's shape and appearance, it is sufficient to use a single safety sign. [In that case] the sitting and arriving individuals inform each other that there is no enemy surveillance. The sign may be keys, beads, a newspaper, or a scarf. The two parties would agree on moving it in a special way so as not to attract the attention of those present.

If the two individuals do not know one another, they should do the following:

a. The initial sign for becoming acquainted may be that both of them wear a certain type of clothing or carry a certain item. These signs should be appropriate for the place, easily identified, and meet the purpose. The initial sign for becoming acquainted does not [fully] identify one person by another. It does that at a rate of 30%.

b. Safety Signal: It is given by the individual sitting in. the meeting location to inform the second individual that the place is safe. The second person would reply through signals to inform the first that he is not being monitored. The signals are agreed upon previously and should not cause suspicion.

c. A second signal for getting acquainted is one in which the arriving person uses while sitting down. That signal may be a certain clause, a word, a sentence, or a gesture agreed upon previously, and should not cause suspicion for those who hear it or see it.

B. The Stage of the Meeting [itself]:

The following measures should be taken:
1. Caution during the meeting.

2. Not acting unnaturally during the meeting in order not to raise suspicion.

3. Not talking with either loud or very low voices ([should be] moderate).

4. Not writing anything that has to do with the meeting.

5. Agreeing on a security plan in case the enemy raids the location.

C. After the Meeting:

The following measures should be taken:
1. Not departing together, but each one separately.

2. Not heading directly to the main road but through secondary ones.

3. Not leaving anything in the meeting place that might indicate the identity or nature of those who met.

Meeting in-person has disadvantages, such as:
1. Allowing the enemy to capture those who are meeting.

2. Allowing them [the enemy] to take pictures of those who are meeting, record their conversation, and gather evidence against them.

3. Revealing the appearance of the commander to the other person. However, that may be avoided by taking the previously mentioned measures such as disguising himself well and changing his appearance (glasses, wig, etc.).

Third Means

The Messenger

This is an intermediary between the sender and the receiver. The messenger should possess all characteristics mentioned in the first chapter regarding the Military Organization's member.

These are the security measures that a messenger should take:

1. Knowledge of the person to whom he will deliver the message.

2. Agreement on special signals, exact date, and specific time.

3. Selecting a public street or place that does not raise suspicion.

4. Going through a secondary road that does not have check points.

5. Using public transportation (train, bus,...) and disembarking before the main station.

   Likewise, embarking should not be done at the main station either, were there are a lot of security personnel and informants.

6. Complete knowledge of the location to which he is going.

Fourth Means

Letters

This means (letters) may be used as a method of communication between members and the Organization provided that the following security measures are taken:

1. It is forbidden to write any secret information in the letter. If one must do so, the writing should be done in general terms.

2. The letter should not be mailed from a post office close to the sender's residence, but from a distant one.

3. The letter should not be sent directly to the receiver's address but to an inconspicuous location where there are many workers from your country. Afterwards, the letter will be forwarded to the intended receiver. (This is regarding the overseas-bound letter).

4. The sender's name and address on the envelope should be fictitious. In case the letters and their contents are discovered, the security apparatus would not be able to determine his [the sender's] name and address.

5. The envelope should not be transparent so as to reveal the letter inside.

6. The enclosed pages should not be many, so as not to raise suspicion.

7. The receiver's address should be written clearly so that the letter would not be returned.

8. Paying the post office box fees should not be forgotten.

Fifth Means

Facsimile and Wireless

Considering its modest capabilities and the pursuit by the security apparatus of its members and forces, the Islamic Military Organization cannot obtain these devices. In case the Organization is able to obtain them, firm security measures should be taken to secure communication between the members in the country and the command outside.

These measures are:

1. The duration of transmission should not exceed five minutes in order to prevent the enemy from pinpointing the device location.

2. The device should be placed in a location with high wireless frequency, such as close to a TV station, embassies, and consulates in order to prevent the enemy from identifying its location.

3. The brother, using the wireless device to contact his command outside the country, should disguise his voice.

4. The time of communication should be carefully specified.

5. The frequency should be changed from time to time.

6. The device should be frequently moved from one location to another.

7. Do not reveal your location to the entity for which you report.

8. The conversation should be in general terms so as not to raise suspicion."[13]

In terms of other communication methods, this time directed at the United States, video tapes from high ranking terrorist leaders are distributed not infrequently. These videos contain messages directed at influencing Americans in their thinking, their politics, and may be used to communicate with other terrorist groups in code.

The Internet is also used by terrorists to convey their messages. For example, on May 14, 2007, Abu Kandahar and Roslan al-Shami used the internet to send a five-part message to Americans. In the message they discussed a number of near-simultaneous attacks in various cities using nuclear weapons hidden in trucks. They named the cities of New York, Los Angeles, and a city in Florida, suspected to be Orlando (due to its proximity to the space center). At the approximate same time they would initiate attacks in other cities, including Seattle, Washington, DC, and oil cities in Texas.

The writers further discussed the economic damage and number of casualties. While appearing to be serious in nature, these types of communications typically are designed to create fear rather than be an actual attack. What is important though, is to understand that terrorists, particularly al Qaeda, are known to state what their intentions are prior to actually doing the attack.

With all this in mind, the United States has, and continues to intercept communications across the globe. Electronic means, including the internet, phones, and radios have not proven inaccessible to American technology. One of the only ways communication has been successful, at least in part, by terrorist organizations, is by the use of runners, people who travel from one place to another to deliver messages and information.

Chapter 7

Transportation Means Used

911 Operator: "911. What is your emergency?"
Caller: "I'm watching what appears to be someone
stealing a car, a Department of Transportation
vehicle. It's happening right now at..."

In their ongoing efforts to plan and execute attacks terrorist groups utilize a variety of vehicles. There have been numerous reports of stolen cars, trucks, and heavy tractor-trailer combinations. While there is no direct nexus to terrorists stealing these vehicles, they are associated with the potential types of attacks they'd like to carry out. In addition, law enforcement, fire, and EMS should be acutely aware of the potential theft of emergency vehicles, as well as first responder uniforms and equipment.

Much information has been shared regarding these possibilities so the operational security undertaken by first responders typically is not a large scale issue. What is more important is that law enforcement and other first response organizations identify and share such information with private sector agencies that have similar operations. Law enforcement should also, as time and ability exist, assist the private sector, where necessary, with the development of their own operational security.

With this in mind, an examination of historic terrorist attacks provides law enforcement and community members with the information on the strategies and methodologies to understand what types of attacks may be in the future and the potential to stop them before they occur. Within recent memory, attacks include:

- **Oklahoma City Murrah Federal Building**
  Domestic terrorists rented a Ryder truck, filled it with explosives and detonated the vehicle bomb in front of the building.

- **1993 World Trade Center attack**
  International terrorists rented a Ryder truck, filled it with explosives, and detonated it after parking it in the underground garage.

- **Iraq**
  Vehicle bombs have evolved significantly, from the use of passenger cars, to small trucks, to larger trucks, to cement mixers. In addition to the terrorists learning how much explosive to deploy in what type of vehicle for what type of operation to achieve maximum effect, they are now learning how to deploy chemicals in the explosives. There have been a number of attacks using chlorine with the explosives.

While the successes desired have not been achieved additional attacks are used to learn how to properly manage chemicals with explosives. The United States should expect this type of attack within the foreseeable future.

Various reports provide information that while the application of chlorine bombs in Iraq have not been as successful as desired, terrorists continually learn and adapt, therefore the attackers will continue to develop and refine their devices to maximize the amount and placement of explosives and chemicals, achieve a much higher number of casualties and damage.

The deployment of these vehicle bombs to determine how to perfect them is invaluable training for the terrorists. It reinforces the premise that they are a determined and deadly foe. In the US, more than 13 million tons of chlorine are used every year. To deploy these devices in the United States, first responders and citizens alike should be aware of their historic use of stolen or modified emergency vehicles, driven by terrorists dressed as emergency responders.

Again, the referral to the al Qaeda Training Manual provides invaluable intelligence for first responders and citizens alike. Their Fifth Lesson regarding transportation includes the following:

"Transportation Means:

The members of the Organization may move from one location to another using one of the following means:
    a. Public transportation,
    b. Private transportation

Security Measures That Should Be Observed in Public Transportation

1. One should select public transportation that is not subject to frequent checking along the way, such as crowded trains or public buses.

2. Boarding should be done at a secondary station, as main stations undergo more careful surveillance. Likewise, embarkment should not be done at main stations.

3. The cover should match the general appearance (tourist bus, first-class train, second-class train, etc.).

4. The existence of documents supporting the cover.

5. Placing important luggage among the passengers' luggage without identifying the one who placed it. If it is discovered, its owner would not be arrested. In trains, it [the luggage] should be placed in a different car than that of its owner.

6. The brother traveling on a "special mission" should not get involved in religious issues (advocating good and denouncing evil) or day-to-day matters (seat reservation,...).

7. The brother traveling on a mission should not arrive in the [destination] country at night because then travelers are few, and there are [search] parties and check points along the way.

8. When cabs are used, conversation of any kind should not be started with the driver because many cab drivers work for the security apparatus.

9. The brother should exercise extreme caution and apply all security measures to the members.

Security Measures that Should be Observed in Private Transportation

Private transportation includes: cars, motorcycles

A. Cars and motorcycles used in overt activity:
1. One should possess the proper permit and not violate traffic rules in order to avoid trouble with the police.

2. The location of the vehicle should be secure so that the security apparatus would not confiscate it.

3. The vehicle make and model should be appropriate for the brother's cover.

4. The vehicle should not be used in special military operations unless the Organization has no other choice.

B. Cars and motorcycles used in covert activity:
1. Attention should be given to permits and [obeying] the traffic rules in order to avoid trouble and reveal their actual mission.

2. The vehicle should not be left in suspicious places (deserts, mountains, etc.). If it must be, then the work should be performed at suitable times when no one would keep close watch or follow it.

3. The vehicle should be purchased using forged documents so that getting to its owners would be prevented once it is discovered.

4. For the sake of continuity, have only one brother in charge of selling.

5. While parking somewhere, one should be in a position to move quickly and flee in case of danger.

6. The car or motorcycle color should be changed before the operation and returned to the original after the operation.

7. The license plate number and county name should be falsified. Further, the digits should be numerous in order to prevent anyone from spotting and memorizing it.

8. The operation vehicle should not be taken to large gasoline stations so that it would not be detected by the security apparatus."[14]

Terrorists obtain vehicles through a variety of means. Some may buy them, use them, and discard or sell them. Others may steal them. Law enforcement, citizens, and the mass media should be aware of thefts of vehicles, particularly emergency vehicles like police likes, fire aid vehicles, and ambulances. The more common way terrorists obtain vehicles is to rent or lease them. The first World Trade Center bombing in 1993 involved a rented van. One of the terrorists was identified when he returned to the rental company to get his $400 payment back.

The Oklahoma City bombing was done using a rented truck. Other plots, interdicted before becoming operational, would have used limousines to attack financial institutions on the east coast. Quite simply, terrorists will use whatever vehicle for an attack that is necessary to complete it. Land, sea, and air transportation will be used as they see fit.

Chapter 8

Identifying Terrorist Financing

Once again, the al Qaeda Manual provides excellent guidance on how terrorists finance an operation. Money laundering, charities, robberies, burglaries, and other seemingly legitimate operations are commonly used. One example used more recently has been amassing and selling cigarettes for profit. This author was recently involved in the investigation of a terrorist organization laundering money after raising millions of dollars through a charity co-sponsored by a major transnational company.

"Financial security precautions:

1. Dividing operational funds into two parts. One part is to be invested in projects that offer financial return, and the other is to be saved and not spent except during operations.

2. Not placing operational funds (all) in one place.

3. Not telling the Organization members about the location of the funds.

4. Having proper protection while carrying large amounts of money.

5. Leaving the money with non-members and `spending it as needed."[15]

Identifying Paper Falsification

Terrorists commonly use forged identification with various aliases or iterations of their names. There may be more than a couple of dozen variations on their name, any of which may have identification associated with it. The iterations may involve interchanging last name with first, or variations of middle names or titles. The al Qaeda Manual, Third Lesson, provides an excellent overview of their methodologies and security precautions.

"Forged Documents (Identity Cards, Record Books, Passports)

The following security precautions should be taken:
1. Keeping the passport in a safe place so it would not be seized by the security apparatus, and the brother it belongs to would have to negotiate its return (I'll give you your passport if you give me information).

2. All documents of the undercover brother, such as identify cards and passport, should be falsified.

3. When the undercover brother is traveling with a certain identity card or passport, he should know all pertinent information such as the name, profession, and place of residence.

4. The brother who has special work status (commander, communication link...) should have more than one identity card and passport. He should learn the content of each, the nature of

the indicated profession, and the dialect of the residence area listed in the document.

5. The photograph of the brother in these documents should be without a beard. It is preferable that the brother's public photograph on these documents be also without a beard. If he already has one document showing a photograph with a beard, he should replace it.

6. When using an identity document in different names, no more than one such document should be carried at one time.

7. The validity of falsified travel documents should always be confirmed.

8. All falsification matters should be carried out through the command and not haphazardly (procedure control).

9. Married brothers should not add their wives to their passports.

10. When a brother is carrying the forged passport of a certain country, he should not travel to that country. It is easy to detect forgery at the airport, and the dialect of the brother is different from that of the people from that country."[16]

Chapter 9

Land Attack Characteristics

This chapter will discuss extensively tactics and methods used by terrorists to plan and execute attacks. Land-based attacks will typically include suicide bombers using improvised explosive devices, VBIEDS, Chemical, bacteriological, or radiological VBIEDS. They likely will apply the extensive lessons learned in Iraq to attacks in the US. Law enforcement, working with American communities should follow the type, scale, and methods of those attacks.

The preferred methodology for land based attacks by terrorists is the use of explosives. Vehicle borne improvised explosive devices (VBIEDS) are the majority of instruments, and terrorist groups have become experts at building, deploying, and detonating them to maximum effect. Their talents include building devices that are formed and shaped specifically to target military vehicles, and they have practiced attacking law enforcement in their training. The second most prominent explosive device is that used by the suicide bomber, wearing a vest containing explosives and other materials or projectiles.

These devices are extremely dangerous as they are essentially self guided devices capable of being delivered exactly where the attacker wants it to go. Many thousands of innocent people have been killed by these devices, and the successes and evolution of tactics and the devices themselves have continued to escalate.

Among the previously mentioned characteristics, citizens should be aware of the following traits for an impending suicide bombing:

- The bombers may utilize their final time preparing a will – usually a video tape;
- Contacting family members to say good-bye;
- Eliminating any evidence related to the attack or their identity;
- Prepare a list of the 70 names their attack will assure a place in heaven.

In addition, the suicide bomber, as the attack nears, will likely be seen substantially less as he prepares his final time. There is the possibility that other suicide attackers may gather in one location just prior to the attack. Finally, many attackers will appear to be either increasingly nervous or much happier and at peace as the attack nears.

With land and sea characteristics, the majority of tactics and strategies are similar, with the exception of the type of vehicle used. For land attacks using a VBIED, much research has shown that the typical car used as a bomb may contain between 500 and 1,000 pounds of explosives. This will produce a large-scale explosion, capable of fatalities within several hundred feet and damage or injury up to blocks away. People should be aware of cars that look weighed down with heavy loads, have wiring inside the passenger compartment, or large boxes or bags of materials.

Trucks and vans will hold considerably more explosives and the same characteristics will apply. Terrorists, however, have and continue to evolve these vehicle bombs to maximize their success in approaching and detonating the bomb. People need to stay a great distance away from these vehicles and notify law enforcement immediately. Take care not to use cellular phone within several hundred feet of the potential vehicle. If the explosion has occurred, stay way from the area as there is a substantial risk of a second, third, or fourth vehicle or device in the area designed to kill first responders.

In addition, Americans and law enforcement should be aware that terrorists, in their pre-operational planning, have likely tried to identify locations responders will use as command posts and staging areas. Quite simply citizens need to stay away from the area of an attack as additional targeting in the area likely has occurred. To be in the area, even with the good intention of trying to help responders, may create even more difficulty and burden on them as they now try to protect you.

Chapter 10

Sea Attack Characteristics

Imagine you are on your dream vacation, a cruise ship in a sunny, warm part of the globe. As the ship nears or leaves a port of call you are on deck and watch a 20-foot boat approach the ship. There are a couple of people aboard and they are waving and smiling at the people lining the deck. As the boat gets closer to the ship it is warned off, yet keeps approaching. As it gets to a point alongside the ship...

The difference with a waterborne attack is that its targets and approached are limited to vessels and water. The same tactics and strategies will be used, with the exception that responders need to be aware of far less visible attacks coming from underwater. Primary targets include ferries and cruise ships. Container ships may be used to smuggle illegal or dangerous materials and personnel into the country.

A definition of maritime terrorism has been crafted by the Council for Security Cooperation in the Asia Pacific Working Group:

"...the undertaking of terrorist acts and activities within the maritime environment, using or against vessels or fixed platforms at sea or in port, or against any one of their passengers or personnel, against coastal facilities or settlements, including tourist resorts, port areas, and port towns or cities.

"The sophistication, expense, and training to carry out maritime terrorism necessitates considerable overhead. It would require terrorist organizations to acquire appropriate vessels, mariner skills, and specialist weapons / explosive capabilities."[17]

Abdul al-Rahim al-Nashiri, one of the responsible parties for the USS Cole bombing, used extensive pre-operational intelligence to identify and attack the ship. His agents rented apartments overlooking the harbor and surveilled numerous Navy ships to determine when the ships would arrive, how long they would be in the harbor refueling, and when and how to attack them. Their plans followed the seven signs of terrorism, the attack characteristics being essentially the same as those of a land or air attack.

The one failure in the original attack was that they did not conduct a dry run. In their case, the original target was the USS Sullivans, nine months prior to the attack on the USS Cole. The Sullivans was targeted not only due to its military significance, but to its symbolism.

In World War II five Sullivan brothers were killed on the same ship. The US government changed its policies to not allow family members in the same theater of war, and honored the Sullivan family by naming this destroyer after them. The same surveillance and other steps were followed, but when the USS Sullivans steamed in to the harbor, they loaded their boat with explosives and on putting it in the water it sunk because it was too heavy with explosives.

The USS Sullivans left before they could resurrect the boat. Knowing that other American warships would enter the harbor they started the cycle again and ultimately attacked the Cole with the same boat and same explosives from the failed attack on the USS Sullivans, killing and injuring dozens of American sailors as they sat at lunch.

Several months following the attack on the Cole, the terrorists launched an attack on a very large crude oil freighter, the MV Limburg. Although the attack did not result in large numbers of fatalities, it did cause sufficient damage to the ship to release 90,000 barrels of crude oil into the sea. The same tactics were utilized in this attack.

Because of these attacks, ships, in particular military ships, increased security substantially, making them harder to attack. Because of this increased security, terrorists have shifted their emphasis to softer targets such as ferries and cruise ships. A super ferry in the Philippines was attacked with explosives placed at a key location inside the boat, resulting in sinking the craft with considerable loss of life. As mentioned before, the ferry systems in the US have been extensively scouted, and the impact of an attack on any of them would result in considerable impacts.

Chapter 11

Air Attack Characteristics

Although America itself and its interests were sub-jected to numbers of terrorist attacks, the country as a whole did not truly awaken to the nature of the threat until 9/11. The use of commercial aircraft as flying explo-sive devices, to be taken to targets of their choosing, pro-duced extensive security modifications to commercial air service.

Several other air-based attacks have been interdicted, clearly showing the terrorist's ongoing interest in using aircraft to initiate attacks. The original hijackings involved small numbers of terrorists who aggressively took control of the planes, killing passengers or flight attendants to get the attention of the passengers. Once done they led the passengers to believe they would be returning to airports to negotiate demands.

Given that most hijackings led to essentially peaceful conclusions, the passengers complied with demands of the hijackers, believing they would survive by doing so, and all were killed when the planes impacted the build-ings. One plane did not reach its target after the passen-gers learned of the attacks and tried to re-take the plane.

In subsequent attempts to use airliners, explosives were smuggled aboard in shoes, in various cosmetic liquid form, in baby formula, and in watches, children's toys, and stuffed animals. In some cases, tests of security during a potential dry run on airliners involved a dozen or more potential hijackers. Their actions caused considerable alarm among flight crews and passengers, resulting in their removal from a plane in one case, and the diverting of flights to nearby airports in others.

The behaviors often include changing seats prior to takeoff and refusal to return to their assigned seats (test of security), lengthy durations in restrooms, at times refusing to come out (test of security and test of timing to see how long they could remain in the facility without being approached).

Other actions include loud praying to Allah while seated or moving around the plane, taking carry-on luggage into a restroom, occupying a restroom by more than one person – all designed to test the reaction of flight crews and passengers.

Characteristics of terrorist attacks continually evolve; they learn from mistakes and prior failures. Law enforcement and airline security must interact closely with civilian passengers, sharing information about tactics, and encouraging immediate reporting when suspicious activities occur.

Chapter 12

The Public and the Battle Against Terrorism

During the 1980's and 1990's, the American public was largely unaware of, and unconcerned about, international terrorism. Although American interests overseas had been frequently targeted and numbers of Americans had been killed, little attention was paid because it hadn't happened here. Americans believed that because of our distance from those countries we were not seriously at risk.

In 1993 the World Trade Center was bombed, resulting in fatalities and many injuries. Most Americans watching the news viewed the pictures of black smoke coming out of the garage and occupants of the buildings being escorted out, some with soot and other injuries. No pictures were shown of the considerable damage to the structures or that there was a near collapse of the towers, which the attack was designed to do. It was identified as a terrorist attack, but little attention was paid to it.

In the eight years following that attack, more Americans and more American interests were killed and damaged in ongoing attacks against our interests abroad.

On 9/11 citizens of the United States watched the attacks in real time, watched some 3,000 of their friends, neighbors, and family members, as well as the first responders who tried to save them, all die. Because of those attacks, Americans changed the way they think and operate.

Making It Difficult for Terrorists

First responders also changed operations, adding intelligence capability, and interaction with one another went to new levels. Awareness became a critical element of safety and prevention. The Seven Signs of Terrorism is reaching more people and cooperation with law enforcement has resulted in stopping a number of attacks. Because of this, and the military destroying terrorist training camps overseas, terrorists are finding it increasingly difficult to complete attacks with the ease they previously experienced.

More and more citizens are getting involved in the battle against terrorism and the successes are mounting. The partnership between law enforcement and their communities is growing faster as a result of the attacks on our country. Citizens are reporting suspicious activities and have provided law enforcement with the ability to actually stop pending terrorist attacks within the United States. They are developing new methodologies to assist first responders and citizens alike to identify terrorists and criminals in their communities.

Training to Help Your Neighbors During the Next Disaster

One of the more effective programs first responders are teaching their communities is FEMA's Community Emergency Response Teams (CERT). This program is designed to prepare communities and individuals for both natural and man-made disasters. The premise is that with a disaster, government resources – police, fire, EMS – will essentially be overwhelmed with activities and emergencies for a period of time. The program partners these government services with their communities to build a level of preparedness and individual response far beyond that of the norm. Many communities across the United States have been trained and others are lined up to receive it. This, in turn, provides first responders with substantially fewer non-emergency issues and allows them to focus on critical problems.

Could There Be Simple Solutions?

If all you had to do to stop a terrorist was learn how to view and describe a face accurately, would you take the time to learn how? There is a simple and profoundly successful method of doing just that.

"...this marks the beginning of a new way for the public to think about helping to solve crime. We will utilize our trained memory to instantly recognize and identify.... terrorists and alert law enforcement,"[18] said Dr. Donna Schwontkowski, author of the book, *Million Dollar Memory for Names and Faces, released recently.* (See www.MillionDollarMemory.net)

In pilot studies where volunteers were taught how to recognize specific characteristics found on faces, their ability to remember the details and accurately imagine a face seen improved up to four times. Even police officers improved their skills dramatically. One of the volunteers, a police artist, was later able to fine tune her sketches so much that it resulted in a 3-year-old unsolved case being solved in a matter of hours after the sketch was released to the public.

"There's a lot more on the face than just eyebrows, eyes, a nose and a mouth. Tuning into the details opens up a whole new world and you begin seeing faces for the first time in your life. The average person sees faces like an 11-year-old does, but with fun identification training, the amount of detail you see on a face helps to differentiate faces, even when those faces appear with disguises," said Dr. Schwontkowski.

With a way to remember and describe faces of suspicious individuals, any citizen can use this simple method to aid in identifying potential terrorists and help interdict attacks. It is through the interaction of good people with their police that a number of terrorist attacks have already been stopped in the United States.

Chapter 13

Legislation in the Battle Against Terrorism

Prior to 1993 there were few laws that specifically addressed terrorist attacks. Now, there is array of federal statutes addressing terrorism, including laws introduced for the use of weapons of mass destruction.

Recent legislation was also passed protecting people who report suspicious activities – this as a consequence of airline passengers and flight crew reporting suspicious behaviors aboard a domestic US flight. The passengers and crew were sued for doing so, and legislation passed to protect against this type of litigation. Legislation introduced in Congress in 2007 to protect corporations from lawsuits while assisting the government remains unpassed as of this writing.

Other laws enacted since 9/11 include the Financial Terrorism Act of 2001, which deals with investigating terrorism funding and freezing assets of terrorist groups. Laws increasing security (via the Transportation Security Administration) have been successfully implemented, and the often used and discussed US Patriot Act, expanding law enforcement powers was established. Additional laws regarding intelligence were added also.

Other legislation enacted to protect America from terrorism include the Security and Accountability at Every Port Act (SAFE Port Act) requiring the 22 major American ports to have the capability to scan for radiation on vessels and containers entering American ports. Subsets include the Customs Trade Partnership Against Terrorism Act (CT-PAT) and Container Security Initiative. Other laws include border fencing, a contentious act to be sure, enhanced pipeline safety, cyber-terrorism (a case occurred on March 13th, 2008 where the government required the removal of a jihadist site on American servers that proposed attacking the United States.

The Effective Counterterrorism Act of 1996 set penalties for providing support to terrorists and terrorist organizations. The FISA Act (the Foreign Intelligence Surveillance Act of 1978) has been used in gathering information specific to terrorist planning and identification of terrorists. Although an act creating disagreement in the US government, and among many citizens, it has proven highly successful when applied. A great deal of intelligence has been acquired and used to stop attacks inside and outside the United States.

The Department of Homeland Security was created following the 9/11 attacks and enormous resources applied in the battle against terrorism. Of the 22 departments under the DHS umbrella, one example that stands out among many is the Transportation Safety Administration (TSA), an agency most Americans have encountered at one time or another. Although an inconvenience the TSA successes are numerous.

Presidential Decision Directives and Executive Orders have been let with the intent of addressing national security and the enhancement of the safety of the public and its infrastructure.

The US Patriot Act has been the single most effective set of laws in addressing terrorism and terrorist acts. Its specific sections set into law the following elements:

- Giving federal law enforcement and intelligence officer greater temporary authority to gather and share evidence, particularly with respect to wire and other electronic communications;

- Amends federal money laundering laws, particularly those involving overseas financial activities;

- Creates new federal crimes, increases the penalties for existing federal crimes, and adjusts existing federal criminal procedure, particularly with respect to acts of terrorism

- Modifies immigration law, increasing the ability of federal authorities to prevent foreign terrorists from entering the US, to detain foreign terrorist suspects, to deport foreign terrorists, and to mitigate the adverse immigration consequences for the foreign victims of 9/11, and

- Authorize appropriations to enhance the capacity of immigration, law enforcement, and intelligence agencies to more effectively respond to the threats of terrorism.[19]

Chapter 14

Response to an Attack

This chapter has conducted extensive discussions of the problems the community and first responders likely will encounter. There are other considerations to understand and apply in order to enhance the chances for survivability, as well as begin to address the wide array of issues they will confront.

"Most law enforcement experts agree that a patrol officer is the most likely person to identify and potentially confront a suicide bomber. We must train patrol officers in the most unthinkable scenarios they have ever faced."[23]

- Suicide bombers, especially on foot, will very likely have a surveillance team in the vicinity.

  Their role is multi-faceted. First, they are present to assure the attack is carried out. They may have the capability to remotely detonate the device if the bomber hesitates or changes his mind.

  Second, they are there to insure that law enforcement does not interdict the attack. They will make efforts to eliminate officers to protect their bombers.

  Third, they will be present to attack first responders who arrive after the fact. Look for these people.

- The same characteristics will apply to an attack on land, sea or air, so anyone trying to stop an attack or respond to one must pay close attention to the surroundings and people in the area, as well as be aware of possible devices.

- First responders and community members should have considerable understanding of the scale and magnitude of a bombing, be it a vehicle borne device or a suicide bomber. Responders and bystanders should expect an extensive and disturbing scene, and be prepared to react accordingly.

- In responding to an attack, officers, fire fighters, and emergency medical personnel should carefully consider whether they want to proceed immediately into the scene. While there will be damage and casualties, by entering the scene without assessing possibilities or the landscape for potential secondary attackers, places the responders at considerable additional risk. Community members need to stay away from the scene and let responders get and maintain control without the additional burden of too many people wanting to assist.

- Also, while responding to an event of any scale, responders historically will place a command post to direct response actions from. Those responsible for setting the location for the command post, staging areas, and other critical locations must consider that the terrorists have likely scouted those sites as well and may have been set up to destroy responders in those locations as well. As a community member you can assist responders by being aware of unusual people or events in those areas, and making a rapid report.

- Responders and members of the community should have a fundamental understanding of the effects of various sizes and types of explosive or other devices, and deploy accordingly to maximize safety. Minimum safe distances should be known by all citizens, not just the responders. They should also know that if a device is present it can be detonated remotely.

- Consider the possibility of chemical, biological, or radiological materials disseminated by an explosion. If an explosion occurs, consider immediate questions, such as which way the wind is blowing and react accordingly.

- Consider the probability of bloodborne pathogens at any such scene. Terrorists have used attackers infected with various diseases. Projectiles in the explosive device are often coated with pathogens or such material as rat poison (an anti-coagulant) to increase casualty rates.

- Understand, ideally, in advance, the tactics, strategies, and philosophies of the terrorists. Understand what may be seen or be confronted with. Being present at or near an attack is not the time to begin to think about what needs to be done or how to react.

Chapter 15

Tactics and Terror

One of the best examples involving negotiations with terrorists is the seizure of a school in Beslan, in Russia. Prior cases, including aircraft hijackings, the 1972 Olympics, the Russian theater incident, clearly show that traditional negotiation techniques used by law enforcement may not be successful in a terrorist takeover event. As an example, the Beslan school incident is described here, and again, the *al Qaeda Manual* provides guidance to the terrorist philosophy regarding such events.

Al Qaeda Manual – "Islam does not coincide or make a truce with unbelief, but rather confronts it. The confrontation Islam calls for with these godless and apostate regimes does not know Socratic debates, Platonic ideals, nor Aristoltelian diplomacy. But it knows the dialogue of bullets, the ideals of assassination, bombing and destruction, and the diplomacy of the cannon and machine gun."[20]

This language, and the large number of ongoing threats made against the United States lends itself to the premise that terrorists are serious about what they say, particularly since they have been repeatedly carrying out those threats.

The Beslan School Siege

A case in point involves the terrorist seizure of a school in Beslan in Russia. On September 1, 2004 30 heavily armed terrorists took control of a school, taking hundreds of school children and adults hostage. The situation continued for nearly three days and resulted in the deaths of 344 civilians, 172 of them children, with hundreds more being injured. The initial attack included more than 1,300 hostages. They were herded into the school's gymnasium and kept seated there while the terrorist strung explosives all around them. During this time the terrorists killed some 20 male hostages, the biggest males, and those who appeared to be in authority positions, in efforts to reduce potential risk to themselves.

During the second day the terrorists released 26 women and small children to negotiators, which was taken as a sign of progress by the negotiators. On the third day, an explosion occurred – there is disagreement on who did it – and gunfire followed. Government forces initiated action against the school and the terrorists activated bombs in the gym, destroying it and many of the hostages; some of the terrorists were killed as well.

The investigation of this incident revealed that the terrorist, after taking the hostages and setting up the explosives around them, systematically executed anyone they believed was a potential threat – as mentioned, large males or those perceived to be leaders or in leadership positions. Once done, they began to barricade the gym against the attack they know would come. They created corridors in the school to the gym the troops would be required to use to get in – specifically designed to maximize the casualties of the troops. It was also believed the hostage takers did not intend to survive and intended the hostages would be killed as well.

The Moscow Theatre Takeover

A second example involves a terrorist event in Moscow, Russia in 2002. 40 terrorists seized the theater with some 850 customers inside. The demands of the terrorists were unreasonable and after two days Russian Special Forces entered the theater after reports the hostages were being killed. Similar tactics were employed in this incident as Beslan. Most of the terrorists were killed, as were more than 129 hostages.

Presuming these reports to be true, it may effectively negate the use of traditional law enforcement methodologies for dealing with hostage situations involving terrorists. If the terrorists never intend to release the hostages and force law enforcement to engage them, it will be on their terms, in a manner they choose, in a situation they have designed. The advantages are theirs.

Law enforcement agencies must address such circumstances through policy and procedures; they must include educational elements for the general public on these types of events and what to expect.

Rules of Engagement
What are they?

Also, government agencies, especially first responders, emphasizing law enforcement, must address the rules of engagement under these types of extremely difficult circumstances. What are the expectations of the public when confronting extraordinary situations where the risk is very high, and outcomes rarely positive?

The rules certainly have to be visited, openly discussed, and policy and procedure created to address them. The events first responders may encounter will offer challenges beyond the norm and the public needs to understand what their representatives are confronted with.

For example, assume the city has a Fourth of July parade and there has been intelligence that such gatherings maybe be a target for a suicide bomb attack. In response the department adds additional officers, a more visible presence, and what plans they believe will be deployed if an attack occurs.

During the parade, one of the officers, while walking through the crowd observes a suspicious person, meeting the appearance of a potential suicide bomber. All the characteristics are present. The individual is standing in the middle of the crowd. The officer needs to do something. What should be done – really?

Should the officer confront the person? If so, will the person detonate the explosives, killing bystanders and the officer? Should the officer engage with force, including deadly force? What has the person actually done, other than appear to be a potential bomber? What if he turns out not to be? What should the officer do?

These discussions and others about the tactics and strategies employed by terrorists must occur now, and policy and procedure developed to address them that is both reasonable and defendable. "It is the terrorist's strategy to undermine public confidence in the ability of the authorities to protect and defend citizens."

The Israelis have been dealing with this problem for years. Their advice to law enforcement has been to teach officers what to do the moment of an attack or the attempt. Prevention begins with the officer on the street, who is forced to make the instant life or death decisions affecting citizens nearby. Rigorous training is required for identifying a potential bomber, confronting the suspect, the mitigation of the situation and preservation of the crime scene whether the bomb detonates or not. The officer must have the authority to take action without waiting for supervisor approval."[21]

Response to Suicide/Homicide Bombers

The community, its police, the military, and intelligence agencies can take steps that work from the outside in, beginning far in time and distance from a potential attack and ending at the moment and the site of an actual attack. Although the importance of these steps is widely recognized, they have been implemented only unevenly across the United States. An article in Atlantic Monthly in 2003 provides first responders with a set of general guidelines to consider. They are included here:

- "Understand the terrorists' operational environment. Know their modus operandi and targeting patterns. Suicide bombers are rarely lone outlaws; they are preceded by long logistical trails.

  Focus not just on suspected bombers but on the infrastructure required to launch and sustain suicide-bombing campaigns. This is the essential spadework. It will be for naught, however, if concerted efforts are not made to circulate this information quickly and systematically among federal, state, and local authorities.

- "Develop strong, confidence-building ties with the communities from which terrorists are most likely to come, and mount communications campaigns to eradicate support from these communities. The most effective and useful intelligence comes from places where terrorists conceal themselves and seek to establish and hide their infrastructure. Law-enforcement officers should actively encourage and cultivate cooperation in a non-threatening way.

- "Encourage businesses from which terrorists can obtain bomb-making components to alert authorities if they notice large purchases of, for example, ammonium nitrate fertilizer; pipes, batteries, and wires; or chemicals commonly used to fabricate explosives. Information about customers who simply inquire about any of these materials can also be extremely useful to the police.

- "Force terrorists to pay more attention to their own organizational security than to planning and carrying out attacks. The greatest benefit is in disrupting pre-attack operations. Given the highly fluid, international threat the United States faces, counterterrorism units, dedicated to identifying and targeting the intelligence-gathering and reconnaissance activities of terrorist organizations, should be established here within existing law-enforcement agencies.

  These units should be especially aware of places where organizations frequently recruit new members and the bombers themselves, such as community centers, social clubs, schools, and religious institutions.

- "Make sure ordinary materials don't become shrapnel. Some steps to build up physical defenses were taken after 9/11—reinforcing park benches, erecting Jersey barriers around vulnerable buildings, and the like. More are needed, such as ensuring that windows on buses and subway cars are shatterproof, and that seats and other accoutrements are not easily dislodged or splintered. Israel has had to learn to examine every element of its public infrastructure. Israeli buses and bus shelters are austere for a reason.

- "Teach law-enforcement personnel what to do at the moment of an attack or an attempt.

Prevention comes first from the cop on the beat, who will be forced to make instant life-and-death decisions affecting those nearby.

Rigorous training is needed for identifying a potential suicide bomber, confronting a suspect, and responding and securing the area around the attack site in the event of an explosion. Is the officer authorized to take action on sighting a suspected bomber, or must a supervisor or special unit be called first?

Policies and procedures must be established. In the aftermath of a blast the police must determine whether emergency medical crews and firefighters may enter the site; concerns about a follow-up attack can dictate that first responders be held back until the area is secured. The ability to make such lightning determinations requires training—and, tragically, experience. We can learn from foreign countries with long experience of suicide bombings, such as Israel and Sri Lanka, and also from our own responses in the past to other types of terrorist attacks."[22]

Chapter 16

Conclusion

Community members, in addition to their first responders need to take seriously the ongoing threats being made against the United States. The country is involved in a war with an enemy unlike any in the history of America – one that is clearly and directly telling America what it is going to do, and is doing it. To ignore such threats is to create enormous risk. "Americans need to recognize that we underestimated bin Laden's motivation, complexity, and determination.

The United States has never had an enemy who has more clearly, calmly, and articulately expressed his hatred for America and his intention to destroy our country by war or die trying. For five years in media interviews, public statements, and letters to the press, bin Laden told us that he meant to defeat the United States and that he would attack – and urge others to attack – US military and civilian targets both in the United States and abroad. In response, the United States never seemed to take bin Laden too seriously, let alone accept the fact that our nation was in the path of real danger."[24] The author also states that "bin Laden unambiguously pledges to use weapons of mass destruction".[25]

The evidence of a forthcoming attack cannot be expressed more clearly and our communities, not just the first responders, must be aware of the type and scale of potential attacks, and must be prepared to conduct preventive operations, as well as prepare to respond appropriately.

"The United States will remain the jihad's primary target. In targeting the United States, al Qaeda will kill as many Americans as possible in as many attacks as it can carefully prepare and execute. Al Qaeda is clearly building up to the point where it will use a chemical, biological, radiological, or nuclear (CBRN) weapon."[26]

Although Americans have many essential responsibilities, and first responders have many other important and clear duties, terrorism should be included among the most critical issues and discussions with citizens, business owners, and educational institutions should be occurring. Intelligence and information development and sharing is absolutely essential, and most law enforcement agencies are involved.

In partnering with the community, all completed educational programs such as CERT (FEMA's Community Emergency Response Teams – of which a large number of Americans have been trained – more are necessary) provide more eyes and ears for first responders, further enhancing information gathering. This, in turn, provides the information necessary to target hardening, driving potential attackers to softer targets.

Knowing that terrorists are specifically targeting first responders, if they enter the scene to help the victims, there is a probability they will be attacked and possibly killed by secondary devices or people. If they don't enter the scene, but instead attempt to isolate and contain it, while waiting for specially trained experts to enter and clear the scene, some of the victims in the scene may not survive.

The argument on the one hand is that responders are trained to react to a crisis and assist those victims, to save lives and mitigate further problems. On the other, if they do react in this manner and some or all are killed or neutralized, they have lost the ability to assist in either case. Departments must engage in these conversations and arrive at policies, procedures, and protocols that are in the best interests of their communities and their responders, and community members need to understand the type and magnitude of decisions responders will be confronted with. Everyone may be sure that the terrorists have done the planning, knowing what the responses historically have been.

Suicide terror is evolving as an art and science and in its sophistication. Community members, teaming with their first responders can do no less in identifying such problems, preparing for them and learning how to inter-dict them before they happen.

Bob Mahoney, a retired 24- year veteran of the FBI with experience in multiple major terrorism incidents, including having been present in the World Trade Center on 9/11, makes a compelling statement for consideration.

"In an age where it is realized that destroying hijacked commercial airliners may be necessary, where vaccines for pandemic disease may need to be rationed, and weapons of mass destruction might be used in our communities, the traditional military concept of "acceptable losses" being visited upon the civilian population becomes an important issue for discussion, policy, planning, and operations of governmental entities at all levels. It is an issue with multiple dynamics and of singularly significant consequences that has yet to receive the level of discourse it requires." Mahoney is an expert to be sure, to be heard.

In addition to his extensive work at the World Trade Center on and after 9/11, he was appointed General Manager for Security Programs for the Port Authority of New York and New Jersey, and was a core member for the Lower Manhattan Counterterrorism Advisory Team, tasked with developing the Master Security Plan for the new World Trade Center. Here is a resource with the knowledge and actual experiences for citizens and first responders to hear – and pay attention to.

The United States is a team and when it comes together in times if need it works, profoundly. This is an issue Americans need to get their arms around and mitigate, now. This is an enemy of America, one not the historic type of enemy the country has decisively handled in the past. This one is educated, knowledgeable, and has the patience and wherewithal to studiously plan attacks designed to inflict massive casualties and destroy the economy.

For those who choose to believe that a form of negotiation or appeasement is the solution, they only need conduct even the shallowest research to learn that such approaches to the more radical fundamentalists has proven fatal in most cases. As stated previously, this enemy clearly stated its intent to destroy the United States, has told the country what it will do, and has been doing it.

Read the many statements made by these people regarding the destruction of the country, then look at the actions taken. They have literally been at war for fourteen centuries and will be at war until judgment day. This will not stop until either they are defeated, or we are.

They have a defined plan which they are following, and they strongly believe in it. In following the goals of the radical Islamic fundamentalists, their first goal is the re-establishment of the righteous caliphate, which dates to approximately the ninth century – its boundaries are shown on the next page.

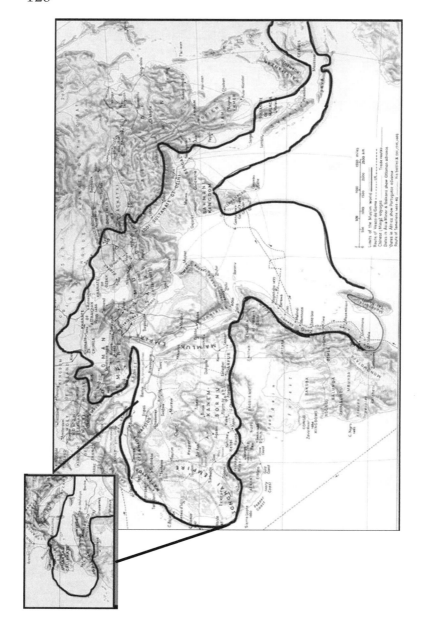

After reviewing the boundaries of the caliphate compare them with the terrorist attack patterns in the next graphic. Radical fundamentalists are actually trying to re-establish those boundaries. Al Qaeda, for example, is present in 60 countries and in conjunction with other fundamentalist groups, has long-term plans of creating a global caliphate, one under their version of what Islam should look like. (See page 128.)

Since 9/11 the radical Islamic fundamentalist groups have committed more than 10,000 attacks that have resulted in the injuries of hundreds of thousands and the deaths of tens of thousands, mostly innocent men, women, and children. This is the only religion (interpreted by the radicals) that propagates the deaths of others to achieve heaven. We have been warned.

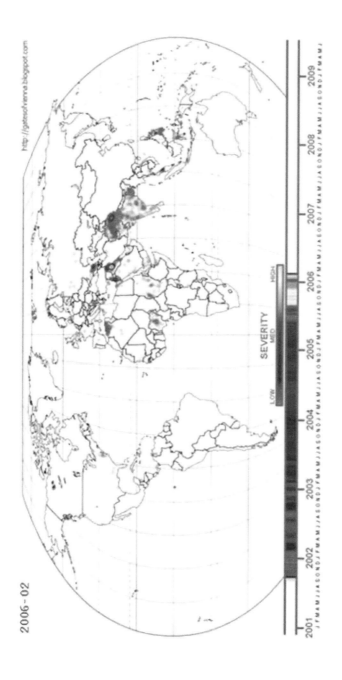

Footnotes

1   "The Terrorist Threat to the US Homeland", July 2007

2   Fred Burton and Scott Stewart, "Al Qaeda and the Strategic Threat to the US Homeland", July 25, 2007

3   Bobby Ghosh, "Inside the Mind of a Suicide Bomber", Time Magazine, June 26, 2005

4   Adam Fosson, "The Globalization of Martyrdom: Cause and Effect", July 2007

5   Ibid

6   Ibid

7   Ibid

8   Scott Gerwehr and Sara Daly, "Al Qaeda: Terrorist Recruitment and Selection", 2002

9   Don Van Natta and Desmond B. Ondon, NY Times, March 16, 2003

10   John S. Pistole, FBI Assistant Director of Counterterrorism, Congressional Testimony, October 2003

11   *Al Qaeda Training Manual*, Lesson 2

12   *Al Qaeda Training Manual*, Lesson 4

13   *Al Qaeda Training Manual*, Fifth Lesson

14   Ibid

15   *Al Qaeda Training Manual*, Third Lesson

16   Ibid

17   Akiva J. Lorenz, "Al Qaeda's Maritime Threat"

18   Schwontkowski, Dr. Donna, *Million Dollar Memory for Names and Faces*, Million Dollar Memory Publications, 2005, page 2

19   CRS Report for Congress, Terrorism: Section by Section Analysis of the USA PATRIOT Act,

130

December 10, 2001.Charles Doyle, American Law Division.

20 *Al Qaeda Training Manual*, Introduction

21 Response to Suicide/Homicide Bomber Policies and Training, Tactical Security Network, Inc., 2006.

22 Bruce Hoffman, "The Logic of Suicide Terrorism", Atlantic Monthly, (June 2003)

23 Police Executive Research Forum, "Patrol-Level Response to a Suicide Bomb Threat: Guidelines for Consideration", April 2007

24 Anonymous, Through Our Enemies' Eyes, Brassey's, Inc. (2002), page xi

25 Ibid

26 Ibid

References

Excellent Internet resources, updated daily in most cases and capable of research:

www.terrorism.com
www.stratfor.com
www.intelcenter.com
www.memri.org
www.thereligionofpeace.com

Bibliography

Anonymous. Through Our Enemies' Eyes. Dulles, VA, Brassey's, Inc., 2003.

Evans, Mike. *The Final Move Beyond Iraq*, Lake Mary, FL, Frontline. 2007.

Safa, Reza F. *Inside Islam*. Lake Mary, FL, Frontline, 1996.

Schwontkowski, Dr. Donna. *Million Dollar Memory for Names and Faces*. Carmichael, CA, Million Dollar Memory Publications, 2005, www.MillionDollarMemory.net

Quick Order Form

(Telephone Orders: Call 425-275-7665
(Have your credit card ready)

E-mail Orders: bcooper193@gmail.com
+ Mail Orders: 3-Star Publishing
              5829 Chennault Beach Drive
              Mukilteo, WA 98275

Please send the following:

☐ Suicide Terror: Confronting the Threat
☐ Terrorism Information Manual

Please send me more information on:

☐ Speaking/Seminars   ☐ Consultations

Name: _____

Address: _____

City: _____ State: _____ Zip:_____

Phone:(_____)_____

E-mail: _____

Payment by: Check Credit Card: Visa   Amer Express
Card #: _____ Exp Date:_____
Name on card: _____

Bill Cooper
Police Chief (ret)

"An outstanding professional speaker"

Recognized by as a speaker who captivates his audiences, Bill provides information and knowledge on a variety of topics that are both powerful and useful.

To invite Bill to speak at your conference, meeting, or school, contact:

Bill Cooper
(425) 275-7665
bcooper193@gmail.com

Rave Reviews from Audiences

"It's about time that a presentation focuses on the biggest threat, as real and primal a concern.... We need this emphasis on what is stalking us as a civilization."

"Very, very knowledgeable presenter, and very impressive. Provided and excellent knowledge base to motivate people to become proactive in their communities to develop and implement response strategies. Bill was a wealth of information. Thank you for having him speak."

"As always Bill Cooper does an awesome job. Keep him coming back."

"The entire program was valuable. Each part builds on the next. Outstanding and very thought provoking. Would look forward to having additional opportunities to attend his future presentations."

"I was very impressed with your background and current position, but what I was most impressed with was how down to earth you were and the common sense approach to life you have in general."

"Bill Cooper has experience and personal presence. He is able to evaluate his audience and bring his program together to reach the scale of the class."

"The information was useful and applicable and the instructor charismatic."